THE PROPHETS II

THE PROPHETS II

Copyright © 1995 by Abingdon Press

This book is printed on recycled, acid-free paper.

Library of Congress Cataloging-in-Publication Data

The Storyteller's companion to the Bible.
    Includes indexes.
    Contents: v. 1. Genesis—v. 2. Exodus-Joshua—[etc.]—v. 7. The Prophets.

    1. Bible—Paraphrases, English. 2. Bible—Criticism, interpretation, etc. I. Williams,
Michael E. (Michael Edward), 1950-
BS550.2.S764   1991   220.9'505   90-26289
ISBN 0-687-39670-0 (v. 1 : alk. paper)
ISBN 0-687-39671-9 (v. 2 : alk. paper)
ISBN 0-687-39672-7 (v. 3 : alk. paper)
ISBN 0-687-39674-3 (v. 4 : alk. paper)
ISBN 0-687-39675-1 (v. 5 : alk. paper)
ISBN 0-687-00120-X (v. 7 : alk. paper)

95 96 97 98 99 00 01 02 03 04 — 10 9 8 7 6 5 4 3 2 1

MANUFACTURED IN THE UNITED STATES OF AMERICA

The Storyteller's Companion to the Bible

Michael E. Williams, editor
VOLUME SEVEN

THE PROPHETS II

Abingdon Press
Nashville

For
Margaret
Sarah
and
Elizabeth

(M. E. W.)

To
Maria-Kristina
and
Tara
for whom stories have meaning

(J. J. S.)

Contributors

John J. Schmitt earned his Ph.D. from the University of Chicago in Biblical Studies. He is Associate Professor in the Department of Theology, Marquette University in Milwaukee, Wisconsin. His first book was *Isaiah and His Interpreters* (Paulist Press, 1986). His second will be a reediting of various articles, *The Israelite City as Woman: A Biblical Image and Its Implications* (Sheffield Academic Press).

Heather Murray Elkins teaches liturgy and preaching at the Theological Seminary of Drew University. She is a popular preacher and workshop leader. Her book *Worshiping Women* was published in 1994 by Abingdon Press.

Beth A. Richardson is assistant editor of *alive now!* In addition to telling stories and miming, she frequently leads workshops for survivors of sexual trauma.

Michael E. Williams is one of the pastors at Belle Meade United Methodist Church in Nashville, Tennessee. He earned his Ph.D. in oral interpretation from Northwestern University and previously directed the Office of Preaching for The United Methodist Church.

Contents

A Storyteller's Companion

Michael E. Williams

This volume, Prophets II, like the previous six in the Storyteller's Companion to the Bible Series, is written for anyone interested in telling Bible stories. Pastors who encounter readings in the lectionary from the prophetic tradition or who choose to preach on prophetic texts will find this volume particularly helpful as they prepare to put the flesh and blood of a sermon on the skeleton provided by a prophetic utterance. If preaching is to help the listener participate in the world of the Scriptures, then telling stories that make the teachings of the thinkers of our faith tradition come alive is imperative.

In addition, leaders of Bible studies may be called upon to "explain" the meaning of a prophetic saying. What better way to answer a call for explanation than the ways the ancient rabbis and sages did, by telling a story? The first six volumes have been used for personal Bible study by many individuals looking for alternate resources for enriching their knowledge of Scripture. It may also be that parents or grandparents will want to tell stories that flesh out some bit of traditional wisdom as they act as the first, and perhaps most significant, teachers in their families.

We live in what some call the information age, and we truly have more facts about a greater variety of subjects at our fingertips than during any previous time in history. To gather many bits of information without seeing any pattern in which they have meaning for us is a very trivial pursuit, as the name of the game suggests. We might say that to have knowledge rather than just an assortment of facts means that we know the *why* behind the *what*. This is often provided by the system of shared values within a society. The words of the prophets still challenge all our trivial pursuits.

The experience of exile is not limited to the ancient world. In the history of North America, the treatment of Native Americans, especially on the Trail of Tears for the Cherokee people in the early nineteenth century, parallels the experience of the exiles of old.

More recently, all we need to do is look at the morning newspaper or watch the evening news broadcast to view the devastation of a people faced by violence in their homeland. In Bosnia, Rwanda, and Haiti we have seen, in recent times, populations decimated by violence. The survivors run for their very lives, but instead of emigrating to the safety of other countries, these exiles too often find no welcome anywhere.

We have also experienced return and restoration among Palestinians in Gaza and the West Bank. The problems of establishing stable government leadership and a society free from turmoil after years of absence of stability and repression—even terrorism—are as much a part of our modern experience as they were for the people of God to whom the prophets of the exile spoke.

The storyteller must realize that exile can be experienced from many perspectives. How many times have we sent people to "Babylon" in an attempt to destroy their culture or assert that our culture is superior to the native culture? We must hear the cries of the exiles and God's promises to them.

The Stories

While we attempt in this volume to be comprehensive in our approach to the prophets of the exile and the postexilic period, we obviously are not able to include them all. We have included the vast majority of texts that appear in *The Revised Common Lectionary,* 1992 (the most inclusive so far). But, in addition, we have gone far beyond the scope of these lectionaries to include stories that make a significant contribution to the biblical prophetic tradition as a whole.

If you do not find one of your favorite passages of Scripture in this collection, there is no need for you to despair. Much of the information you will learn from the comments on the stories that are included immediately after each story can be transferred to other texts. This will allow you to use your creativity more fully.

The translation from which the printed texts in The Storyteller's Companion are taken is *The Revised English Bible.* You may wish to compare the readings here with your favorite translation or with several other versions. Your familiarity with several translations of the Bible will enrich the telling of biblical stories, especially for those storytellers who do not read scripture in the original language, so we encourage you to work from various translations.

Comments on the Stories

John Schmitt, the author of the "Comments on the Story" sections, teaches in the Department of Theology at Marquette University. His comments offer an insight into those "spokespersons for God" who comforted and challenged a people who were in exile and later, in the process of returning and rebuilding their deserted homeland.

The specific contribution you will make to the preparation for telling one of these stories is your knowledge of your audience, knowing what will draw them into each story. Your familiarity with the audience will help you to know what aspects of the story to focus on, and will help you to be more creative in developing your own story line. You can take the information John Schmitt offers and shape a telling of the story that will be appropriate to the needs and life experiences of your group of listeners. Only you can know where in the lives of those in your congregation, class, or family a story will strike a chord, turn on a light, or heal a hurt. For more information on how to prepare a story for a specific group of listeners, refer to the chapter "Learning to Tell Bible Stories: A Self-directed Workshop" on pages 23-24.

Retelling the Stories

As a storyteller, you will contribute something of your own personality and understanding of the Bible and your listeners to the telling of a story based on a biblical text. There is no one right way to accomplish this task. While The Storyteller's Companion includes a sample retelling of each story, these retellings are only examples of one way a story may be told. You may choose to tell it very differently.

The retellings are intended to free your imagination for telling and not to limit you to any one form. Some retellings here are fairly straightforward recountings of a text. Others choose a character or characters from whose point of view to tell the story. Some retellings even place the story in the modern setting. We hope they will offer you a sample of the vast number of ways Bible stories can come to life in storytelling.

The goal of each retelling is to help our listeners to hear the wisdom of the lesson as if for the first time and to see the world of the lesson as something new and fresh. We are grateful for the imaginations of the storytellers who provided the retellings for this volume:

Heather Murray Elkins teaches liturgy and preaching at the Theological Seminary of Drew University. She is a popular preacher and workshop leader. Her book *Worshiping Women* was published by Abingdon Press (1995).

Beth A. Richardson is assistant editor of *alive now!* In addition to telling stories and miming, she frequently leads workshops for the survivors of sexual abuse trauma.

Midrashim

If you ask a rabbi a question, you are likely to get a story for an answer. This reflects a wisdom that knows truth to be irreducible to a one-two-three answer. Truth is embodied in events as they happen and in persons as they relate to each other and to God. This kind of truth is best experienced in stories and concrete images. Perhaps no book is a better example of this storied truth telling than the Bible.

The most unique contribution The Storyteller's Companion makes to the art of biblical storytelling is to include the stories and sayings of the ancient rabbis related to the sayings of the prophets of the exile and post-exilic period. These stories are called *midrashim* (the singular is *midrash*), from a Hebrew word that means "to go in search of." When the rabbis went in search of the relevance of these already "old, old stories" for their time, they returned with questions. Those questions generated stories that stand alongside the Scripture passages and interpret them in ways that children and adults alike are better able to understand.

The midrashim included here came from several sources, and I have retold and adapted them for inclusion here. You will find these midrashim in boxed text in the retelling of each story, placed near the part of the story to which they most closely relate. As you retell the story, you may wish to include one or more of the midrashim at these points in the story or at other appropriate places. For more information, refer to the chapter "What Are Midrashim, and What Are They Doing Here?" on pages 19-21.

You will probably not want to read this volume in The Storyteller's Companion to the Bible Series from front to back as you would most books. It is not designed to be read that way. One way to make effective use of this volume would be to read first John Schmitt's "Introduction to Stories of Exile and Prophets," on pages 15-17, and his comments on each of the stories and the introduction to midrash. Then choose a story that you wish to tell. This may be a story from an upcoming Sunday of the lectionary or the church school curriculum, or it may simply be a story that captures your interest. Once you have chosen the story, work through the short workshop on storytelling ("Learning to Tell Bible Stories: A Self-directed Workshop," pages 23-24), using the story you chose as your content. Practice telling your story alone until you feel comfortable.

As you tell the story to your group, notice which parts seem to touch your hearers the most. Take note of any questions or comments they may have, and incorporate these thoughts into any future stories.

Use the retelling provided with the story as a guide, but do not feel obligated to simply repeat it. Because you know your audience, you should tell the story for your hearers in your own way. You may choose to include the midrashim with your retelling, or you may tell them afterward, or you may choose not to include them at all. In any case, you are about to take part in one of the most ancient experiences people do in community: offering the gift of God's story so that it touches our story today.

Introduction to Stories of Exile and Prophets

John J. Schmitt

The selections in this volume of The Storyteller's Companion to the Bible series come from the exilic and post-exilic times of the biblical story. The leaders among the people of Jerusalem were deported to Babylon, there to engage in the struggle to maintain the community's identity, to keep alive its treasured traditions, and perhaps to broaden its self-definition.

The exile was a crisis. In this period, the people of the Bible felt challenged to test and validate their tradition, to look back on the past, to evaluate the actions of previous generations—and their own. To see the past, to reflect on the present, and to gaze into the future—this was the current task. It was a time to rethink and reevaluate some of the standard ideas and principles of their predecessors and of their heritage.

The religious leaders in the exile and post-exilic times, as presented in the Bible, are prophets. These individuals help the exiles fit this new experience into the stories and ideas from the past, thereby creating the next chapters of the stories.

Two entities with different stories dominate the thoughts of the prophets of this time. These entities had been images by which previous generations had also thought of themselves and of their relation to God. These two entities, or images, were the people and the city. The people of Israel have a story of the people that differs from the story of the city. The reader must notice these differences in order to appreciate them.

The story of Israel the people is well known to readers because it is the one that is explicitly narrated. The biblical books of Genesis–2 Kings and into Ezra and Nehemiah tell the story with Abraham as the beginning of the story. Israel is a promise, a seed, a hope in the narratives of the ancestors. But eventually, Israel's time in the womb is over, and the "child" emerges in birth at the time of departure from Egyptian bondage. The time of independence from the divine parent is the wilderness wanderings. Israel, the sibling of the mature peoples around the area, is now readied by Moses' instructions in the book of Deuteronomy.

The story of Jerusalem the city is not as explicitly told. The city's story is usually only alluded to by many different references in passages that are not narrative; they are often lyric. The city is chosen by God. Built by God, it is the dwelling place of God. God loves the city so much that protection is given the

15

city against any enemy. Eventually, the city will be glorified and will receive the honor it deserves.

These stories differ in a variety of ways. The most immediate difference is the same as the most basic human distinction among human beings: that of sex, or gender. Of course, here it is a matter of grammatical gender, but this lowly linguistic phenomenon seems to have been a major influence on the images used for the two. "The people" is a masculine construction, often referred to as the "son of God," while the city is spoken of in feminine terms, often referred to as "daughter." The relation between a masculine God and a feminine city naturally differs from the relation between the same God and a masculine people. Both relationships receive appropriate metaphors.

The city's relation to God is depicted in a variety of images. But the basic themes are clear: divine foundation, divine nurture, divine indwelling, and divine protection. When these themes are converted into masculine-feminine relations, there is an interesting variety. God is seen as the father of the city, sometimes without qualification, and sometimes as a foster parent. The daughter sometimes is cast out of the custody of the paternal home, but at other times is found sexually attractive. In certain settings, the woman becomes the wife of God. When she is a mother, the mother is often very fruitful in offspring. The distant hope—sometimes a vivid vision—is that the city will be glorified in her children, that the fulfillment of her hope will be realized and she will receive all the honor that her status deserves.

The two stories really are not in contradiction to each other. The story of the city need not exclude the story of the people. Likewise, the story of the people did not necessarily rule out the story of the city.

Many Bible readers, indeed, feel no tensions between the stories because of the differences. Some of the biblical writers present the two stories in such a way that they seem to become one story. But close attention to the Bible's treatment shows that there are two distinct stories.

Both stories are different ways of showing God's love. The city language is a specific way of showing God's interest in the biblical community. Hardly surprising is the ease by which city language is applied as equally to Samaria, the capital of the Northern Kingdom, founded in the ninth century, as it is applied to Jerusalem, the capital of the south, founded a millennium before that. The imagery of the city does differ and is more varied than the imagery of the people. But the two coexist as two options to convey the message, and prophets chose freely to use either one.

These two stories—that of the people and that of the city—had furnished the preexilic prophets with many images and ideas to convey their convictions. Probably all of the eighth-century prophets knew well both stories, but each prophet is memorable for the special use made of the city tradition. Amos speaks of the Virgin of Israel who no longer has the right to the protective paternal home that she formerly experienced. Hosea describes God's divorce of his wife. In both of these examples, eighth-century prophets use the city tradition about the city of Samaria. Once this capital of the Northern Kingdom is established, all the standard imagery of the city tradition can be and is applied to Samaria as it had been to Jerusalem. Even the southern prophet Micah speaks of the harlot's hire that Samaria earned, and Isaiah names Jerusalem a whore.

The times of the exile and the return to the land are certainly critical. The Bible shows that a simple return is not easy, for struggles arise about the leadership and exercise of power. Prophets use all the imagery of the past that can help the people through these crises and into a new assurance.

The two major prophets of this exilic time are Ezekiel and the unnamed prophet whose words now appear in Isaiah 40–55, who is known as Second Isaiah. The two prophets are quite different. Ezekiel was a priest and was deported from Jerusalem to Babylon in the first deportation in 598 B.C.E. Thus he lived in Babylon some ten years before the fall of the city of Jerusalem in 587. He thinks himself well acquainted with the failure of the city in matters religious and ethical. He predicts the fall of the city and lives through it. But once the city has fallen, his view turns to the future, and his message becomes one of hope and restoration.

The anonymous prophet of the exile seems to be a generation (or two) younger than Ezekiel. This nameless prophet speaks little or nothing of the real fall of Jerusalem. Now the need is to convince the exiles of God's decision and imminent activity to free them from captivity in Babylon. Enormous energy and creativity are expended for that purpose. It seems that the effort does not convince many. Some scholars have suggested that Second Isaiah was a woman, for these chapters contain the greatest concentration of feminine images for God.

Of the postexilic prophets in this volume, the one who appears with the greatest number of passages is "Third Isaiah"; the quotation marks appear around the name because many commentators judge that Isaiah 56–66 were not written by simply one person, but that they come from the hands of several different unknown prophets.

The other postexilic writers—Joel, Jonah, Haggai, Malachi, and Baruch—have left us smaller books. These books offer less information about the prophets themselves.

The great variety of material here—images, assertions, hopes—is great. All of the utterances of these prophets of the sixth, fifth, fourth, and maybe even later centuries B.C.E. offer the storyteller rich sources and spurs for retelling and reexperiencing.

What Are Midrashim, and What Are They Doing Here?

Michael E. Williams

Midrash (the plural in Hebrew is *midrashim*) comes from a Hebrew word meaning "to go in search of" or "to inquire." So midrashim resulted when the ancient rabbis went in search of (inquired into) the meaning of the Scriptures for their lives. Midrash is also the name for the process of inquiring into the Scriptures for their meaning.

We might say that midrash is both our encounter with the biblical stories as we seek their meaning for our lives and times and the stories that emerge to express that meaning. Often midrashim do take the form of stories or pieces of stories (at least the ones we will focus on here do). These stories seek to answer questions about and to fill gaps in the biblical stories.

The midrashim drawn from for this volume come from the period 400–1200 C.E. (what is sometimes called A.D.). They were told, in part, to make the prophets' stories and images relevant to a Jewish community that had no homeland, could not hold citizenship in other countries, and experienced hostility and persecution from the outside, including from Christian authorities. Most of these midrashim originated in sermons preached in synagogues, based on the prescribed weekly readings from the Torah (the first five books of the Bible). Others emerged from the popular folk traditions of the Jewish communities. Though they were collected and written during that six-hundred period, there is no way of knowing how long the midrashim had been circulating by word of mouth before someone wrote them down. Some are attributed to rabbis living at the time of Jesus. In fact, certain scholars find evidence that this way of interpreting the Bible has its roots intertwined with the texts of the biblical stories themselves.

I see three basic functions for the midrashim I have selected to be included in this book. The first might be called "filling the gaps." These stories and story fragments answer questions about the biblical stories that the Scripture leaves unanswered. When the rabbis answered such questions, they revealed both their fertile imaginations and their own understanding of God and human beings. Sunday school teachers and college professors will also have encountered these imaginative questions.

The second function of midrash is to draw an analogy. These stories begin with "This may be compared to. . . . " Then the rabbi would tell a contemporary story that exhibited a situation and characters like the biblical story under consideration. You may notice that these stories sometimes bear a resemblance to the parables of Jesus and the *mashal* (parable) form of Jewish teaching.

The third function is to describe an encounter. In these stories someone comes to a rabbi with a question, and the rabbi's response interprets both the biblical story and the situation from which the question emerged.

Why did I choose a predominantly Jewish form of interpretation in this book? First, Christians have too often ignored this ancient and time-honored way to interpret the Bible. Given our Jewish roots and Jesus' heritage, midrash is at least as directly related to our tradition as the Greco-Roman philosophy on which we have depended so heavily for ordering our questions and structuring our theological doctrines.

Second, midrashim provide us with a way of interpreting the Bible that involves the imagination and speaks to our experience. It is also, according to certain scholars, the way the Bible interprets itself.

Third, midrashim provide a model for a community-based, inclusive (even children can imaginatively participate in stories), nonprofessional (you don't have to be a trained theologian) way of interpreting the Bible for our times. In short, we can learn the stories the rabbis told about the scriptures to interpret them for their time. In addition, we can follow the example of the rabbis and learn to tell stories about Bible stories that interpret them for our time.

In addition to these reasons I have a personal appreciation for the Jewish storytelling tradition. My intellectual and artistic interests in Jewish narrative range from the Torah to midrash to hasidic stories to modern writers like Isaac Bashevis Singer and Elie Wiesel.

This is just the first step to reclaiming midrashim for modern tellers of Bible stories, but it is a step. If you want to learn more about midrashim related to the wisdom tradition, you may wish to read the volumes from which those included here were chosen.

Midrash Rabbah, translated by H. Freedman (London: Soncino Press, 1939), is a ten-volume translation of midrashim on a variety of books of the Bible. These references here, which have been paraphrased and adapted, are to chapter and section. The third edition of this work was published in 1983.

Volume one in Louis Ginzberg's classic collection of stories related to biblical texts, *The Legends of the Jews,* translated by Henrietta Szold (Philadelphia: The Jewish Publication Society, 1909 and 1937), still in print, draws from a wide number of sources, including Christian and Islamic traditions. Here this work, again paraphrased and adapted, is listed as Ginzberg, followed by the volume and page number.

A wonderful addition to the library of persons interested in midrashim is Rabbi William G. Braude's translation of Hayim Naham Bialik and Yehoshua

Hana Ravnitzky's *The Book of Legends (Sefer Ha-Aggadah): Legends from the Talmud and Midrash.* References to this work are cited as *Sefer Ha-Aggadah,* followed by the page number and section number.

One more word on midrash: For any given passage of Scripture, several stories or interpretations of various rabbis are presented side by side in collections of midrashim. Those who collected these stories saw no reason to decide which was the one right interpretation. This is also true, we might mention, of those who assembled the canon of the New Testament, who saw no reason to choose among the four very different stories about Rabbi Jesus. The understanding behind these choices is that there need be no single correct interpretation. The Bible is viewed as being so inclusive that it could apply to a range of possible life situations. Therefore, we would expect a variety of interpretations to speak to a variety of life situations. Not only the Bible, but also all of its many possible interpretations, are encompassed by the expansive imagination of God. In fact, Solomon, the wisest of all humans, is reputed by the rabbis to have known three thousand stories for every verse of Scripture and one thousand and five interpretations for every story.

Learning to Tell Bible Stories

A Self-directed Workshop

1. Read the story aloud at least twice. You may choose to read the translation included here or the one you are accustomed to reading. I recommend that you examine at least two translations as you prepare, so you can hear the differences in the way they sound when read aloud.

Do read them *aloud*. Yes, if you are not by yourself, people may give you funny looks, but this really is important. Your ear will hear things about the passage that your eye will miss. Besides, you can't skim when you read aloud. You are forced to take your time, and you might notice aspects of the story that you never saw (or heard) before.

As you read, pay special attention to *where* the story takes place, *when* the story takes place, *who* the characters are, *what* objects are important to the story, and the general *order of events* in the story.

2. Now close your eyes and imagine the story taking place. This is your chance to become a playwright/director or screenwriter/filmmaker because you will experience the story on the stage or screen in your imagination. Enjoy this part of the process. It takes only a few minutes, and the budget is within everybody's reach.

3. Look back at the story briefly to make sure you haven't left out any important people, places, things, or events.

4. Try telling the story. This works better if you have someone to listen (even the family pet will do). You can try speaking aloud to yourself or to an imaginary listener. Afterward ask your listener or yourself what questions arise as a result of this telling. Is the information you need about the people, places, things, or language in the story? Is it appropriate to the age, experiences, and interests of those who will be hearing it? Does the story capture your imagination? One more thing: You don't have to be able to explain the meaning of a story to tell it. In fact, those of the most enduring interest have an element of mystery about them.

5. Read the "Comments on the Story" that John Schmitt has provided for each passage. Are some of your questions answered there? You may wish also to look at a good Bible dictionary for place names, characters, professions, objects, or worlds that you need to learn more about. *The Interpreter's Dictionary of the Bible* (Nashville: Abingdon Press, 1962) is still the most complete source for storytellers.

6. Read the "Retelling the Story" section for the passage you are learning to tell. Does it give you any ideas about how you will tell the story? How would you tell it differently? Would you tell it from another character's point of view? How would that make it a different story? Would you transfer it to a modern setting? What places and characters will you choose to correspond to those in the biblical story? Remember, the retellings that are provided are not meant to be told exactly as they are written here. They are to serve as springboards for your imagination as you develop your telling.

7. Read the midrashim that accompany each retelling. Would you include any of these in your telling? You could introduce them by saying, "This is not in the original story, but the rabbis say. . . . " Do these midrashim respond to any of your questions or relate to any of your life situations or those of your listeners? If so, you might consider using them after the retelling to encourage persons to tell their own stories, which hearing the Bible story has brought to mind. You may even wish to begin creating some modern midrashim of your own or with your listeners.

8. Once you have gotten the elements of the story in mind and have chosen the approach you are going to take in retelling it, you need to practice, practice, practice. Tell the story aloud ten or twenty or fifty times over a period of several days or weeks. Listen as you tell your story. Revise your telling as you go along. Remember that you are not memorizing a text; you are preparing a living event. Each time you tell the story, it will be a little different, because you will be different (if for no other reason than that you have told the story before).

9. The "taste and see" that even the stories of God are good—not all sweet, but good and good for us and for those who hunger to hear.

Call of the Prophet

Isaiah is called to challenge and bring comfort to the people.

The Story

Comfort my people; bring
comfort to them, says your God;
speak kindly to Jerusalem
and proclaim to her
that her term of bondage is served,
her penalty is paid;
for she has received at the LORD's
    hand
double measure for all her sins.
A voice cries:
'Clear a road through the wilderness
    for the LORD,
prepare a highway across the desert
    for our God.
Let every valley be raised,
every mountain and hill be brought
    low,
uneven ground be made smooth,
and steep places become level.
Then will the glory of the LORD be
    revealed
and all mankind together will see it.
The LORD himself has spoken.'
A voice says, 'Proclaim!'

and I asked, 'What shall I proclaim?'
'All mortals are grass,
they last no longer than a wild flower
    of the field.
'The grass withers, the flower fades,
when the blast of the LORD blows on
    them.
Surely the people are grass!
The grass may wither, the flower fade,
but the word of our God will endure
    for ever.'
Climb to a mountaintop,
you that bring good news to Zion;
raise your voice and shout aloud,
you that carry good news to
Jerusalem,
raise it fearlessly;
say to the cities of Judah, 'Your God is
    here!'
Here is the Lord GOD; he is coming in
    might,
coming to rule with powerful arm.
His reward is with him,
his recompense before him.

Comments on the Story

This section of the book of Isaiah opens majestically. Its message of consolation seems capable of consoling the most troubled of persons. Indeed, its message was addressed to people who had been taken from their homes and placed in a foreign land when Jerusalem was conquered and destroyed in 587 B.C.E. Modern critical study of the Bible proposes that one prophet wrote most of Isaiah 40–55, but we do not know who that individual was. Modern tradition calls this prophet in the Babylonian exile Second Isaiah, because these

25

chapters come from a person and a time quite different from the Isaiah of Jerusalem who can be heard in chapters 1–12 or 28–32. This insight, that exiles in Babylon are being addressed in Isaiah 40–55, comes from the twelfth century of the Christian era and the careful readers of that time.

In this reading, the scene is the divine court. God is imagined seated on a throne (as in Isaiah 6) and surrounded by many courtiers. Some of these courtiers are the former gods of the Canaanites, and others are distinct Israelite figures who attend the divine king. Admission to this court of God can make an individual a prophet in Israel, and it is there that a prophet receives a commission and a message.

Many prophets who came before this prophet had been commissioned to preach judgment against a sinful people. Our present prophet might be thought of as the only prophet commissioned solely for consolation. Actually, the opening command, "Comfort, give comfort to my people," is addressed to more than one person. But it is only an individual response that is recorded (v. 6).

The one who is to be consoled in these opening verses is Jerusalem. From the start we see that the story of Jerusalem has influenced this exilic prophet enormously. In fact, analysis shows that the prophet has two sections within chapters 40–55. In the first section (41–48), the main figure, spoken to or about, is Israel. In the second section (49–55), the major figure is Jerusalem/Zion. This passage from the introductory chapter 40 seems cast as a "call narrative," and it serves as an introduction to the combination of the two sections. The first image is Jerusalem.

The voice in verse 3 is one of the court members. Its command to build a highway should be very understandable in the twentieth century. People in almost every country today have seen bulldozers moving mounds of earth to create the superhighways that crisscross the continents on our planet. But the prophet is not alluding to the movement of weapons, merchandise, troops, or even curious travelers. The prophet is probably thinking of the processional walkways used in Babylon for the Babylonian god Marduk and his subordinate deities. But this new highway is for the one, unique God and for those human beings associated with that God. The way is for the return trip to Jerusalem whence they had journeyed to Babylon a generation past. The procession back would, no doubt, be a better procession than anyone could remember or even dream up. Indeed, the event will be so grand that "all flesh" will see it.

The image of the human race as the grass and flower of the field helps the prophet to depict the awe and grandeur of the procession. While the promised return of God and God's people to the city of God is a glorious vision, "all flesh is grass," which withers and its flower fades. This thought of the transitoriness of life, which has played a major role in contemporary thought, probably has haunted the hearts of most human beings over the ages.

The purpose of that saying in Isaiah, however, is not to instill morose feelings. Rather, the fading quality of human beings enhances and gives vivid contrast with the power and durability of the divine Word. It is remarkable that Isaiah 40–55 both begins and ends with reference to the Word of God. Here at Isaiah 40:8, the eternal endurance of the Word is the focus. At 55:11, the effectiveness of that Word is highlighted. This prophet (or an editor) is convinced that what is presented here is truly the Word of God in this situation.

Salvation is near, and the precise form of salvation can be nothing less than return to the holy city. The prophet is versatile in his use of the word *Jerusalem*. Sometimes the word refers to the actual, physical city the people will return to, and sometimes the word is used as a way of addressing the exiles themselves who must be convinced of their imminent (or near-imminent) return home. In verse 9, the grammar allows both uses of the word. Perhaps the easiest reading that employs both uses is this: The prophet foresees the band of exiles returning to their home and addresses them as "Jerusalem" to encourage them to shout ahead to the people in the cities of Judah, including Jerusalem, the good news that God and God's people are now returning.

God comes with a reward—not as God had once come with punishment (v. 1). But this coming of God brings freedom and happiness. The people will find their true joy and fulfillment at last.

Most lectionary readings stop with verse 10, but verse 11 is too interesting and moving to ignore. God's return is truly majestic (and trustworthy). But the majesty does not rule out tenderness. God is depicted as a shepherd who cares for the sheep and helps them move along. The little ones even get carried.

Retelling the Story

Once a woman who had a lovely garden dreamed of a desert. In her dream, she saw herself wandering through a desolate landscape of jagged rocks and barren dust. The sun was scorching, yet the air was bitter cold. She searched the horizon, but it appeared as if she were the only liv-

One rabbi contended that it was God who needed to be comforted rather than the people. He argued that if someone owns a vineyard and thieves enter it and destroy it, who needs the comfort, the vineyard or its owner? Or if someone burns down a house, who needs comforting, the owners of the house or the structure that burned? Just so God's house (the Temple) is burned and God's vineyard (the people) is destroyed. We should be comforting God, not expecting God to comfort us says this particular sage. (*Sefer Ha-Aggadah* 150.20)

27

ing creature in this immensely empty space. There were no landmarks—just sand and rocks and a large cold sun hanging in the middle of the thin blue sky.

The woman considered her choices, then decided to travel in the direction of her left hand. There didn't seem to be any normal sense to geography, such as north or south, east or west. So she simply lifted her left hand and pointed in a direction, which she then followed.

It seemed as if she had traveled for miles, for years even, when she spotted what appeared to be a circle of stones at the base of a mountain. As she drew closer to the stones, feeling the cold and her thirst, she recognized that the stones were part of an ancient well. They were round, like stones from a river, yet they were neatly fitted together in a circle several feet high and several feet wide.

When the woman reached the circle of stones, she leaned over and looked down. To her intense relief, she could see the reflected light of water at the bottom of the well. Her delight gradually faded, however, as she looked for a way to reach the water. She circled the well, looking for a rope or long sticks or anything to hold water. All she found was sand and more sand, sharp rocks and the circle built of smooth river stones.

Despair replaced delight, and she finally sat, exhausted, on the edge of the well. Wrapping her arms around herself to keep out the cold, she closed her eyes and tried not to think of the water she could see and not reach. Miserable and alone, the woman soon found herself talking angrily, complaining bitterly about her thirst and a well with no bucket and a sun that burned hot and cold.

It is said that Isaiah was blessed with a double portion of God's prophetic power. It was God, not another prophet, who had anointed him to preach good news to the poor (Isaiah 61:1). This is the reason we find Isaiah repeating certain words and phrases a second time. His repetition is not just for emphasis, but a reflection of his double blessing. That is why we read, "Comfort ye, comfort ye my people." (*Leviticus Rabbah* 10.2)

Suddenly, from out of nowhere, a voice interrupted her lament. "Water the flowers," the voice said. So startled was the woman that she nearly fell backward into the well. She stood up, scanned the horizon, circled the well, peered under some of the rocks, but could find no source for the voice. Perhaps she had imagined the words, but just as she started to sit down, she heard them again. "Water the flowers." Again, she searched. Again, she found nothing.

Now she was angry. She was thirsty and cold and lonely. There weren't any flowers! There wasn't any rope! She couldn't reach the water—but as she sputtered, the landscape began to change. Out of the sand grew green shoots and leaves. Tens and hundreds and thousands of buds slowly bloomed in front of her startled, angry eyes. Flowers, flowers everywhere, but flowers unlike any she'd ever seen, for as each blossom opened, it seemed to form a face. Some faces seemed familiar; others were unknown, but wherever she looked, there were flowers and faces. They seemed to be waiting, waiting for water, waiting for her. Blooming on their own, yet bending in her direction.

She heard the voice begin again, "Water . . . " and she whirled around, stamped her feet, and shouted down the well, "I can't water the flowers! I don't have a bucket. I don't have a rope. I don't even have a teaspoon! How can I water the flowers?"

She listened. She listened for a long time, but all she could hear in the silence was the sound of the wind, blowing through the sand and the blossoms. And all she could see, leaning over the edge of the well, was the wavering form of her face, reflecting up from an unknown depth. And all she could sense was the weight of wet stones, pressing against her hands. But somewhere, mixed with the fragrance of flowers, she caught the scent of water. *(Heather Murray Elkins)*

Mountaintops were special places of God's presence in the ancient world. It is little surprise that Isaiah is called to the top of a mountain to proclaim his message. Certain sages claim that this was the appropriate place for those who had struggled with God to receive their reward. (*Leviticus Rabbah* 27.2)

Eagles' Wings

Jacob says that nobody loves him, but the prophet encourages the faint-hearted.

The Story

Do you not know, have you not heard,
were you not told long ago,
have you not perceived ever since the world was founded,
that God sits enthroned on the vaulted roof of the world,
and its inhabitants appear as grasshoppers?
He stretches out the skies like a curtain,
spreads them out like a tent to live in;
he reduces the great to naught
and makes earthly rulers as nothing.
Scarcely are they planted, scarcely sown,
scarcely have they taken root in the ground,
before he blows on them and they wither,
and a whirlwind carries them off like chaff.
To whom, then, will you liken me,
whom set up as my equal?
asks the Holy One.
Lift up your eyes to the heavens;
consider who created these,
led out their host one by one,
and summoned each by name.
Through his great might, his strength and power,
not one is missing.
Jacob, why do you complain,
and you, Israel, why do you say,
'My lot is hidden from the LORD,
my cause goes unheeded by my God'?
Do you not know, have you not heard?
The LORD, the eternal God,
creator of earth's farthest bounds,
does not weary or grow faint;
his understanding cannot be fathomed.
He gives vigour to the weary,
new strength to the exhausted.
Young men may grow weary and faint,
even the fittest may stumble and fall;
but those who look to the LORD will win new strength,
they will soar as on eagles' wings;
they will run and not feel faint,
march on and not grow weary.

Comments on the Story

In this last half of the first chapter of "Isaiah of Babylon," we get to see the enthusiasm and exuberance of this prophet. This individual is truly moved by the marvelous news of salvation and return to Jerusalem and is eager to share it. We also get to see certain literary devices the prophet uses to convince the exiles that his message of God's coming liberation is credible.

31

Our reading begins right after the prophet's emphasis on the incomparability of the God who is giving this good news. Nothing at all is like this God. Especially no model or form of god is like the God whom the prophet preaches and whom the exiles are to believe. Now the prophet turns to the idea that the God who wants to deliver them is the God who made the world. The passage begins with a kind of chiding: The people have certainly heard of creation and should now become convinced that the God who created their world can now surely do whatever is needed to bring about their salvation from captivity.

Perhaps some storytellers have been struck by the reference to grasshoppers right in the middle of this elevated speech on creation. Do grasshoppers really carry much theological weight in a prophet's argument? Actually the use of the Hebrew word for this insect is very effective. The prophet has chosen a double word play to get the message through. The word translated "enthroned" (from *yashab*) is related to "inhabitant" (also from *yashab*), and the word rendered "vaulted roof" (*chug*; RSV has "circle") sounds similar to "grasshoppers" (*chugab*). The prophets were predecessors of speechwriters who might employ some trick to get the message out and across. (Some older readers might recall the "nattering nabobs of negativity.")

Another image also might surprise the reader: God "stretches out the skies like a curtain,/ spreads them out like a tent to live in" (v. 22). The imagery has shifted from "vaulted roof" to "tent." The prophet reveals an awareness that the dome of the sky, as the ancients conceived of the sky, was like a tent. It was the tent of meeting where in ancient times God made revelations, where God met with people, and where God planned the next action. This time the next action will be the deliverance of the exiles.

The prophet in verses 23-24 declares that God can overturn anything, reverse any process or event, and certainly reduce any person. In a nice touch, the prophet compares the Babylonian leaders and their actions to the grass of the field, the same image used in the opening scene for the broken and exhausted exiles themselves. God can change all things, can do all that is necessary to free the people.

A final insistence that God can be compared to nothing introduces the idea that even the stars of heaven will have a roll call, preparatory to the moment when God will act. What greater conviction could an ancient person have than to know that the most regular things in life, the stars of the sky, must follow the commands of one's own God?

The passage reaches its goal when Israel is addressed directly. "Jacob" is, of course, simply a different way of referring to the people as "Israel," following the biblical tradition that the ancestor Jacob was renamed Israel. The prophet chides Israel for being timid and untrusting. Israel, in a moment of despondency, had said that God does not care about him.

32

It is not difficult to see why Israel is depicted as saying this. The exile was an enormous disorientation for the people. So many elements of what they had held as essential to their tradition and religion were now gone or inaccessible. No temple, no sacrifice—the very things by which one could reach God no longer existed. Gone too was a reigning king, the person in whose majesty one could see a reflection of the divine. Away from the city of their birth and growing up years, the exiles had little foundation for hope and conviction that their God could still act with power.

The prophet is persistent in his message: God can change all that. Even if the young grow weary and faint, God can and will give them strength and vigor. Trust in the fact that God will change weakness into strength. In a final, irresistible image, the prophet says that the exiles' revivification will feel like being carried on eagles' wings. Running toward the goal of return will not even be felt as a strain. One can almost hear the divine wings as the exiles are being borne aloft to return home.

Retelling the Story

It's not that it was a famous race, you understand. It was a small-time race in a small town that had a lot of time. And it's not that any world records were broken—nothing like that. It's hard enough to do anything but stroll when the July heat descends on the river and the whole Ohio Valley takes a steam bath. And it's not that there haven't been some really fine runners, long-legged golden boys and girls who made it out of town and went on into the world without breaking stride.

It's just that memories tend to get stuck in the unexpected cracks in reality's sidewalk. Something odd trips you up, and you remember that place, those people, whatever was said or not said, done or not done. Memories congregate around those cracks, and then come the stories. These make more memories, and before you know it, the crack turns into a chasm.

The race was a memorial all by itself; each entry fee went to a scholarship dedicated to a young Greek

The creation stories of Genesis tell of the beginnings of the earth and its inhabitants, but do not go into detail about how the creation came to be (except that in the first of the two stories it was spoken into being by God). But Isaiah offers a graphic description of the act of creation when he says that God "stretches out the skies like a curtain, spreads them out like a tent to live in" (Isaiah 40:22b). It seems that God's hospitality reaches throughout the heavens and the earth preparing a tent in which all creation might live. (*Genesis Rabbah* 1.6)

33

god destined for the majors, until some drunk shattered this collective hope into broken bones and glass. It helped to work out our grief in a public way, to outrun the pain held in common. And over the years, the scholarship did help some other winners get out of town in style.

But this particular monument of memories is dedicated to a loser of this race. The unexpected part wasn't the fact that he lost. We expected him to lose. He was only six years old, after all. The armband that his mother put on him flopped around his elbow. He bounced around the starting line with a nervous energy that the neighbors said reminded them of his dad, who had died shortly before his son was born. Seeing him there, outnumbered and outweighed, wasn't the unexpected part. Aaron was a doer, like his dad. This race was worth doing, so Aaron was there.

The mayor talked a little too long and pulled the starting trigger a little too soon, but that was expected. Everybody and anybody was there to run or watch. That, too, was expected. The real drama came from wondering whether the octogenarian optometrist might die this year with his sneakers on, or whether Mr. X would notice how good the former Mrs. X looked in running shorts. And didn't he deserve every wink, running around on her like he did? All sorts of humanity lined up along Main Street, ready to run the good race.

Once the gun went off, all the watchers retreated to porches and lemonade. Well out of the sun, we discussed the route as if it were a marathon. Three times around the town limits. We speculated less about winning, more about just hanging on. The first runner made his appearance down at the corner of the volunteer fire department, home of the only real Christians in town. We scanned the runners as they came by, some with smiles tied neatly as shoes, some already unraveling. Aaron wasn't last. He waved once, but did not smile, fierce and frail all together.

The second round held to the expected; front runners came and went, and we waited for the runners-up. Now heat and stress began to strip away the padded layers of control. The joints of personality were laid bare. Some runners went missing, having surrendered, breathless, on some neighbor's porch. The optometrist was reduced to a stroll, enjoying the view, and Aaron was last, his armband missing, face and fists clenched, nothing to spare.

On the third lap, three golden boys jockeyed for first place. One won by a nose, but all were cheered and properly pounded. Now the serious watching began. Who was left, and what had it cost them to come this far? Mr. X got a few nods, but the ex-Mrs. X was loudly cheered as she finished four steps behind.

When the last runner had rounded the corner, the crowd prepared to celebrate, spilling into the street, closing the gap. A loud whistle parted us open. A small figure was spotted rounding the corner, on his last lap. We gave him room, held back by his too-white face, his too-fixed eyes. Ten yards away, the unexpected happened. One minute he was up, the next he was down, tripped by a lace or a stone or by being just six. He went down, and we watched his mother, to see what she would do. She had first rights to first aid.

She pushed through and bent down to check him, to see that he was all right, whether he wanted to rise on his own. After a count of two heartbeats, she picked him up and turned. She shifted him higher, took a deep breath, and then—well, she carried him over the finish line. Ran him right over the line. You had to be there. It's hard to explain. Just plain normal turned into something else.

Some of the sages suggest that the image of people looking like grasshoppers from God's vantage point does not really include everybody upon whom God gazes. Rather, the wicked are like grasshoppers caught in a bottle, jumping frantically to gain some advantage only to fall back down to the bottom of the pile of their competitors. (*Sefer Ha-Aggadah* 554.172)

We got a glimpse at the heart of things, I guess. We still talk about it, every so often. *(Heather Murray Elkins)*

First Servant Song

God advises the Servant to seek justice with compassion.

The Story

Here is my servant, whom I uphold,
my chosen one, in whom I take
delight!
I have put my spirit on him;
he will establish justice among the
nations.
He will not shout or raise his voice,
or make himself heard in the street.
He will not break a crushed reed
or snuff out a smouldering wick;
unfailingly he will establish justice.
He will never falter or be crushed
until he sets justice on earth,
while coasts and islands await his
teaching.
These are the words of the LORD who
is God,
who created the heavens and
stretched them out,
who fashioned the earth
and everything that grows in it,
giving breath to its people
and life to those who walk on it:
I the LORD have called you with
righteous purpose
and taken you by the hand;
I have formed you, and destined you
to be a light for peoples,
a lamp for nations,
to open eyes that are blind,
to bring captives out of prison,
out of the dungeon where they lie in
darkness.
I am the LORD; the LORD is my name;
I shall not yield my glory to another
god,
nor my praise to any idol.
The earlier prophecies have come to
pass,
and now I declare new things;
before they unfold, I announce them
to you.

Comments on the Story

This passage is the first of the four songs of "the Servant of Yahweh" (Isa. 42:1-4; 49:1-6; 50:4-11; 52:13–53:12). Only within the past century have these four sections of Isaiah 40–66 been separated from the rest of the book for analysis on their own. Some people still think it better not to set them apart from the whole but rather to see them as they relate to the surrounding texts. But many readers, long before this separation was made, felt some tie among these sections, even though they are not a continuous passage in our Bible. One can find a storyline within the songs when they are separated and seen as a sequence. In fact, the four songs present many changes of speakers and addressees, a feature that has led some scholars to stress the dramatic quality of the songs.

37

Isaiah 42:1-9 opens with words of an unidentified speaker. Only in verse 5 is the speaker named: God. The first four verses have God address a general audience, while in the last four verses God speaks directly to the Servant. In God's initial presentation, the role of the Servant is quite remarkable: to bring justice to the nations, to be silent and very caring, yet to concentrate his efforts tirelessly on justice and to have an impact even on what is far distant.

The task, then, is enormous, establishing justice, seemingly for the whole world. The prophet certainly has a great and broad vision in these opening verses. The prophet has international events in mind, both present and future. No doubt the present event is the succession of victories that Cyrus, the leader of the Persians, was experiencing in the eastern edges of the Babylonian Empire. The future event will follow and resemble those and the future military advances of this leader. The culminating victory of Cyrus over Babylon will bring a new order to the world of the prophet and his people.

The power of the prophet's vision must be connected with the idea that the speaker is God. The attributes or activities of God listed here are all related to creation. What God has created includes the heavens and the earth and all that fills them, especially the human beings who live on the earth and receive their very breath from God. This emphasis on creation and the story of creation in Isaiah 40–55 has already been pointed out, so this reappearance simply serves to confirm for Second Isaiah's readers the importance and reliability of God's creative activity.

An investigation of the imagery used by the prophet to sketch the Servant's figure and role finds different combinations of elements in the individual songs. Here, a dominant trait of the servant's depiction is the theme of royalty. Only a king has the major task of assuring and ensuring justice in his kingdom. Even when the required justice seems to be in the cosmic realm, the king is central. This royal connection agrees with the links between ruling and creation elsewhere in the biblical tradition. The Israelite king might possibly have reenacted aspects of creation in the religious rituals. Whether such a ritual really existed, the king did have the awesome and onerous task of maintaining justice.

But the other dimension of the depiction of the Servant in this song is that of prophet. Persons like Elijah and Elisha became prophets when the Spirit of the Lord came upon them. A similar gift of the spirit empowers the Servant for his task as well. Moreover, the Servant is to carry out his duties with the concern and care with which many earlier prophets operated. A particular verbal surprise in this depiction is the same root (*ratsats*) translated in the RSV as a "bruised" reed and the servant who will not "be discouraged." The REB, here more careful than some other translations, uses the same word (meaning "crushed" or "crush") for both. The Servant, then, is identified with those whom he is sent to aid.

One can note that the REB in verse 6 does not have the possibly familiar phrase "a covenant to the people." Rather, the REB renders the words as "a light for peoples." It reads the first word as one coming from an east Semitic root meaning "to shine." The poetic structure suggests this reading. The prophet, who grew up in Babylon, might easily have known that word. (The same phrase occurs in Isa. 49:8.) The Servant is to be a shining light to the nation, to the peoples, and to the world.

Even the "opening of the eyes of the blind" is the kind of miracle that befits a prophet. No healing of sight is recorded in the Hebrew Bible; rather, there the phenomenon is associated with the time of fulfillment. Healings of whole persons, however, are found in the tales of Elijah and Elisha. The next theme, "freeing of captives," appears quite frequently in Isaiah 40–66. The reference is clearly to the exiles in Babylon. The servant is to lead these people back to the city of God's love, Zion.

The last two verses, which extol the uniqueness and glory of God, are part of the larger context of this passage within Isaiah 40–55. It is a court scene where the God of Israel is presenting his own case over against that of the Babylonian gods. Part of Yahweh's justification is his designation of his Servant. But another part of this justification is the argument that only the God of Israel had made predictions that clearly did come true. Now the new predictions of salvation for the exiles are given, and just as surely they will come true.

Retelling the Story

The original identity of the Suffering Servant described in these verses from Isaiah is unknown. Was he the unnamed prophet whose words we now read? Did the prophet describe someone the community knew so well that he did not need to name him? Was this a vision of One who was to come, or someone who had lived as an exile among exiles? We do not know. What we have done with this description is to use it to identify the servant/leader in any time and place whose image matches this stark outline.

One such figure is Abraham Lincoln, whose somber watch over Washington has turned a public building into a shrine. Many of the first-person stories of Lincoln have been forgotten, but there are some that deserve preserving, such as the account of Mrs. La Salle Pickett, wife of the Confederate general who made the charge at Gettysburg.

Legend tells that she was in Rich-

When Isaiah spoke of giving "breath" to the people, many teachers interpreted that to mean "spirit." And when the prophet spoke of God giving "like to those who walk on (the earth)," (Isaiah 42:5*d*) they had a special piece of earth in mind. Many rabbis taught that those who walked even a few steps in the land of Israel were destined to have a portion in the world to come. (*Sefer Ha-Aggadah* 306.13)

mond when her husband fought the battle of Five Forks. Richmond surrendered, and a surging sea of fire swept the city. When news of the battle reached her, it included the report that her husband, General Pickett, had been killed; but she refused to believe it and waited for further news. The day after the fire there was a sharp rap at the door. The servants had all run away. The city was full of Northern troops, and La Salle's environment had not taught her to love them. With her baby in her arms, she opened the door and looked up at a tall, gaunt, sad-faced man in ill-fitting clothes. He asked, "Is this George Pickett's place?"

"Yes, sir," she answered, "but he is not here."

"I know that, ma'am," he replied. "But I just wanted to see the place. I am Abraham Lincoln."

"The President!" she gasped. The stranger shook his head.

"No, ma'am; no, ma'am. Just Abraham Lincoln, George's old friend."

"I am George Pickett's wife, and this is his baby," was all La Salle could say. She had never seen Mr. Lincoln, but she remembered the love and reverence with which her soldier husband had always spoken of him. The baby pushed away from her and reached out his hands to Lincoln, who took the baby into his arms. As he did so, an expression of rapt, almost divine, tenderness and love lighted up his sad face. It was a look never seen on any other countenance. The baby opened his mouth wide and insisted on giving his father's friend a kiss.

As Lincoln gave the little one back to his mother, he shook his finger at the baby playfully and said: "Tell that rascal, your father, that I forgive him for the sake of that kiss and those bright eyes." He turned and went down the steps, talking to himself, and passed out of sight forever. But in La Salle's memory those intensely human eyes, that strong, sad face earned a perpetual abiding place— that face that puzzled all artists, but revealed itself to the intuitions of a child. *(Heather Murray Elkins)*

Several Roman philosophers were involved in a discussion with the Emperor Hadrian. One of the philosophers said he had a matter of some urgency about which he wished to ask the emperor: The questioner's ship was being tossed about on stormy seas and all the merchandise that the man wished to sell was aboard. The emperor offered to send his own ships and sailors to rescue the vessel. No need, said the philosopher, just send some calm winds to ease the storm. The emperor allowed that he had no control over the winds. Hearing this the philosopher quoted Isaiah and assured the emperor that only God could perform such a feat. How the philosopher came to be acquainted with Isaiah or had the audacity to quote the prophet and put the emperor in his place the sages never explain. (*Sefer Ha-Aggadah* 510.52)

God Is Always with You

No matter what the trial, God is with you, has named you, and will deliver you.

The Story

But now, Jacob, this is the word of the LORD,
the word of your Creator,
of him who fashioned you, Israel:
Have no fear, for I have redeemed you;
I call you by name; you are mine.
When you pass through water I shall be with you;
when you pass through rivers they will not overwhelm you;
walk through fire, and you will not be scorched,
through flames, and they will not burn you.
I am the LORD your God,
the Holy One of Israel, your deliverer;
I give Egypt as ransom for you,
Nubia and Seba in exchange for you.
You are more precious to me than the Assyrians;
you are honoured, and I love you.
I would give the Edomites in exchange for you,
and any other people for your life.
Have no fear, for I am with you;
I shall bring your descendants from the east
and gather you from the west.
To the north I shall say, 'Give them up,'
and to the south, 'Do not obstruct them.
Bring my sons and daughters from afar,
bring them back from the ends of the earth:
everyone who bears my name,
all whom I have created, whom I have formed,
whom I have made for my glory.'

Comments on the Story

In this passage, Israel is again addressed directly. The introductory words that identify God as the speaker emphasize that Israel was created by this God who has given Israel a special calling. This application of the biblical teaching of creation to the story of Israel is striking. The prophet leaves nothing to chance or to a vague idea that Israel might have some relation to this God. God created and fashioned Israel. It is somewhat like a Christian's saying, "Jesus died for me." A general statement will not do. The prophet had already stressed general creation, and now an application is made to Israel.

The words that open the divine speech occur frequently in Isaiah 40–66. The

41

assurance "Fear not, for I am with you" has been called by scholars the "priestly salvation oracle," and they claim that it was probably uttered in the religious shrine or site when a troubled person came seeking divine reassurance that things would work out. Here the prophet charged with proclaiming salvation to the exiles almost inevitably uses the kind of address that the exiles or their parents would have remembered from the old days back in Judah. God still has a proclivity to save.

The speech enumerates some of the possible trials that Israel might go through. Nevertheless, God will always be with the people. It is worthwhile to point out that the whole passage addresses Israel in masculine singular. Israel may have more to suffer in the very return home to the land, but God promises to remain with Israel as protection and defense.

The divine speaker is so concerned to convince the Israelites that they can trust him that he insists that he has already shown himself to be Israel's savior by delivering them from bondage in Egypt. This act he views as a kind of comparative valuing or even an economic exchange. Not only does God value Israel more then Egypt but also more than any other peoples the prophet can think of. He names some from both ends of the Fertile Crescent and the neighboring Edom (following the reconstructed text that the REB uses).

The future return of the exiles becomes quite specific by mentioning geographic directions. Both from the east and from the west—the east would be Mesopotamia, including Babylon where the exiles were living; and the west would be the Mediterranean Sea! (One can see the boundless enthusiasm of the prophet, using language that cannot possibly be taken literally.) From the north and from the south—the north could refer to the mythic land whence issue disasters and where the Canaanite gods lived (and also the actual route the exiles would use in the return), while the south was the desert land.

It is interesting to note the versatility of thought that the prophet employs. God says he will bring Israel's descendants (literally "seed") from the east. Then he says he will gather Israel from the west. The Israelites are equated with the offspring of Israel. But then God calls them God's own children, "my sons and daughters." This is an extraordinary claim: The descendants of Israel are God's children.

But the surprises do not stop there. Everyone who is called by this God's name, God will bring back in a universal salvation. (This is one way, at least, of reading the text.) And the surprise continues: "all whom I have created, whom I have formed." This surely can refer to those who at one time did not recognize the God of Israel and now have chosen to claim this God. Conversion to Israel's God and way of life are here implied, and perhaps encouraged.

In verse 7, "everyone who bears my name" is more literally "who is called by my name." Here there is a reference, according to some, to verse 1, where Israel is directly addressed. In such a view, verse 1 really should read, "I call you by *my* name; you are mine." This reading enhances the unity of the passage, since being called by God's name begins and ends the passage. In fact, in most modern translations it is too easy to assume that Israel gets an actual name: "Mine." But this understanding is not allowed by the Hebrew, which stresses possession rather than the giving of a name.

Finally, the motivation might also be surprising: "Whom I have made for my glory." "Glory" has been called one of the themes that tie the whole book of Isaiah together. At least it is an essential part of the theology of the original Isaiah, and that theme appears in many passages of the whole book. God's glory is often that by which God's presence is revealed by physical events. God wants to be with all people.

Retelling the Story

In the early stages of the Civil War, there were prohibitions against recruiting and arming black troops. Countless men of color in the North tried to volunteer, longing to join in the struggle for their own emancipation. The need for troops became critical, but the color bar held, limiting men of color to serving the white officers in the field, or assisting the field physicians.

A story is told of a physician in Pittsburgh who volunteered to serve General Grant's army. He arrived with his medicine and personal gear and was led to a tent where an old man was waiting. The old man promptly saluted the doctor and offered himself as a volunteer.

Zeke, short for Ezekiel, had been a servant in a Boston home for more than sixty years. As the doctor soon learned, Zeke was skilled at repairing anything that was broken, from legs to wheels, and proved to be a gifted preacher. After the doctor and Zeke had mended the bodies of the soldiers to the best of their ability, Zeke took up the work of mending their souls.

After several months in the field, Zeke acquired a copy of an old *First Reader* from a schoolteacher turned soldier. He persuaded the doctor to teach him the alphabet. Hovering

Some sages took God's promise to be with Israel as they passed through the waters to be a reference to an event from an earlier biblical narrative. As Jacob was fleeing from his home and from Esau's anger, he came to a place near Lake Tiberias (the Sea of Galilee) where the water of the Jordan flows into it with a crashing roar. As Jacob hid there Esau cut off his escape route. But God provided a way out for Jacob by digging an escape through the other side of the falls. (*Genesis Rabbah* 76.5)

over the campfire, night after night, Zeke worked at learning the letters. Finally, he learned to spell words of two syllables, and soon after that, he tackled words of three syllables. Wet or dry, hot or cold, night after night, the weary man labored over the pages of the old book.

One day he came on the name "G-O-D" in the reader. It was spelled in capital letters, and he did not recognize the word. He brought his book to the doctor, who said, "Why, Zeke, that is the name of the Great Being that you preach so much about—that is the name of God!"

Some rabbis contended that when the Messiah came the winds would become rivals. The north wind would claim, "I will bring back the exiles of the Northern Kingdom." Then the south wind would boast, "I will return those who were forced from the Southern Kingdom back home." Then God will reconcile the two rivals by bringing all the captives home. (*Numbers Rabbah* 13.2)

Zeke lifted his hands in surprise, and tears came to his eyes. "Is that the name? Is that the way it looks when it gets printed? You can't understand it, Doctor. You always knowed how to read, but I been preachin' about that name all these years, all these years, and now, thank God, thank God, I see it. I know God holds my name, knows my name, writes my name in his book of life. But now, doctor, now these old eyes have lived to see and read the name of God!" *(Heather Murray Elkins)*

The Second Exodus

A foreigner will deliver Israel, and the wilderness will be a paradise.

The Story

This is the word of the LORD,
who opened a way in the sea,
a path through mighty waters,
who drew on chariot and horse to their
destruction,
an army in all its strength;
they lay down, never to rise again;
they were extinguished, snuffed out
like a wick:
Stop dwelling on past events
and brooding over days gone by.
I am about to do something new;
this moment it will unfold.

Can you not perceive it?
Even through the wilderness I shall
make a way,
and paths in the barren desert.
The wild beasts will do me honour,
the wolf and the desert-owl,
for I shall provide water in the
wilderness
and rivers in the barren desert,
where my chosen people may drink,
this people I have formed for myself,
and they will proclaim my praises.

Comments on the Story

This passage is Second Isaiah's fullest reference to Israel's deliverance from Egypt and the awe-filled march through the fearful waters of the Red Sea. The prophet remembers isolated details from the general story of Israel's liberation, in order to assure the exiles that God is going to do a similar thing in their own days.

The first detail is the combination "chariot and horse." Not only are the chariots and horses referred to as perishing because the sea closes in on them, but also God is depicted as drawing the riders of the horses and chariots into the sea for their imminent extermination. One might say that if this depiction were not for a good cause (to convince the people of their own future freedom), this image of God is quite unattractive and inappropriate. The emphasis for the interpreter should fall in the liberation and salvation that God provides rather than on the deviousness of the God depicted in verse 17.

The defeat of the Egyptian forces is presented as complete and permanent. The image of a smoldering wick is used here. The prophet had used it in the first of the Servant Songs. The appearance here, however, is expressed by words different from the Hebrew words in the song. The allusion is subtle, and the interpreter is free to stress it or not.

The prophet insists on the newness of the future event that is being

45

announced. "Don't remember the past; look ahead!" This advice is not merely good psychology. This message is what God is saying through the prophet. The past was good enough, but God can do something better. The past will be outdone by what is going to happen.

The newness so overtakes the prophet that he says this new event is taking place in the midst of things going on. He cries out, "I can just feel it. Can't you?" He wants the reader to have the same conviction and enthusiasm that he has. He is almost like a salesperson who is trying too hard to sell something he perceives as such a great deal you would regret not taking it.

What is this great deal? Why is the prophet trying so hard to convince his contemporaries to take it? This prophet has received a calling to preach the imminent freeing of the captives by God. The problem is that this liberation, this great act of salvation, which will glorify their God of old, will be accomplished by a foreign ruler. This apparent inconsistency seems the major reason why the prophet tries so hard. The news is so good, but the means by which the saving act will be accomplished is a shock. The work will be done by an individual who comes not from the chosen people of the God of Israel but from an unfamiliar people.

The sketchy description of Israel's return to Zion is remarkable. In the Exodus narrative of Israel's coming out of Egypt and trek through the wilderness, God gives the people of Israel what they need for the long and tedious trip to the land of promise. In our passage, Israel will again traverse a wilderness. But now God transforms the wilderness into an inviting land, one that is described as if it will be a joy to go through. The wild beasts of the desert that usually attack people will now honor the God of the people who will be crossing through their land. The dryness of the desert will be no problem, for God will furnish rivers of fresh water to all who might be weary and thirsty.

Israel, in the last verses of the reading, is identified as God's chosen people. Elsewhere in Second Isaiah the verb for "to choose" is used to refer only to the chosen city and the chosen servant. Now it is applied to the people as a whole. Perhaps it is important to recall that three religious communities claim to be the fullness of the people Israel in exile: Jews, Christians, and Muslims.

It is worthwhile to see how this passage fits with the text that immediately follows it. The prophet seems in 43:16-21 to be gearing up for what comes next. In the next passage, 43:22-28, the same chosen people are castigated for their unresponsiveness and infidelity in the past. But God says that even this failure is no obstacle for the divine mercy. "I wipe out your transgressions and remember your sins no more."

Retelling the Story

Israel was a nation that had been uprooted, led into exile and slavery, then returned home by means that appeared miraculous. To tell their stories in an

American way means we need the stories of the peoples who experienced this uprootedness, this long journey home. One such people are the Cherokee, who survived the Trail of Tears, a forced march from the southeastern United States to the territory of Oklahoma. Some of the tribe members escaped and made their way back home, living in the woodlands and swamps, avoiding contact with white settlements.

Over time, the federal government changed its policy and allowed these refugees to resettle the forests they once inhabited as a strong community. Perhaps it requires such a cultural dislocation to produce stories of helpers who lead the lost to return home. Legends of "little people" or "small ones" who rescue those who are lost in the woods can be found throughout Cherokee tribal lore. The old people of the tribe kept the small ones alive through the stories they told. Every so often these small ones would leave clues to their actual presence. Signs of their dancing circle would be found in woodland clearings. Sounds of their drumming would be reported by the very young and old alike. But young adults, educated in the ways of the modern world, do not see the signs or hear the drums.

> When Isaiah speaks of God opening "a way in the sea," some rabbis suggested that it really means that God appointed a period of time each year when it was safe to take a sea voyage. This time of safety in sea travel was between Pentecost and the Feast of Tabernacles. Some sages even told cautionary tales about persons who had attempted voyages at other times and had perished. (*Genesis Rabbah* 5.8 and *Sefer Ha-Aggadah* 770.110)

There is an old story of two children who wandered off while their family was setting up camp in the woods. The girl and her younger brother heard a strange noise in the woods, the sound of drumming. The parents did not seem to notice, so the children went in search of the source of the sound. No matter how close they came to the noise, it always seemed just hidden out of sight, coming from behind a tree or a rock.

The two grew tired of the search, but could not remember which way the camp was, or at what spot they had left the trail, which had been clearly marked. The sunlight was beginning to fade when the girl dis-

> When God (through the prophet) insisted that people, "Stop dwelling on past events and brooding over days gone by" (Isaiah 43:18), it meant that people should not allow ancient defeats and hardships (even slavery in Egypt) to divert their attention from the new things that God was about to do in their midst. (*Sefer Ha-Aggadah* 394.47)

47

covered a small cave with a fire burning brightly at the entrance. Peering in, she could see what looked like small mats rolled and stacked against the cave wall. When she turned to find her brother, he was standing next to a small man, who had his arm around the neck of a large gray wolf.

The small man smiled, and the wolf rubbed its head against the boy's outstretched hand. The children sat beside the fire and were fed something wonderful that they had never seen before and could not describe later. The small man never spoke, but the children were not afraid. After they had rested a while, the man and the wolf led the children back through the woods until they could hear the sound of their mother and father calling their names as they searched for the children.

In the excitement of their discovery, the children did not notice that the little man and the wolf had faded away into the forest. No matter how many times the children tried to explain what they had experienced and who had helped them, no one believed what they said. After a time, even the children doubted their own story. It's just as well. We know our way around this planet. There's no place in the real world for little people who live in caves, walk with wolves, and specialize in leading children home. And everyone knows there's nothing new under the sun. It's even written in the Bible somewhere. *(Heather Murray Elkins)*

Cyrus the Anointed

A Gentile king is ordained by God to deliver Jacob from exile.

The Story

Thus says the LORD to Cyrus his
   anointed,
whom he has taken by the right hand,
subduing nations before him
and stripping kings of their strength;
before whom doors will be opened
and no gates barred:
I myself shall go before you
and level the swelling hills;
I shall break down bronze gates
and cut through iron bars.
I shall give you treasures from dark
   vaults,
and hoards from secret places,
so that you may know that I am the
   LORD,
Israel's God, who calls you by name.
For the sake of Jacob my servant
and Israel my chosen one

I have called you by name
and given you a title, though you have
   not known me.
I am the LORD, and there is none
   other;
apart from me there is no god.
Though you have not known me I shall
   strengthen you,
so that from east to west
all may know there is none besides
   me:
I am the LORD, and there is none
   other;
I make the light, I create the
   darkness;
author alike of wellbeing and woe,
I, the LORD, do all these things.

Comments on the Story

This passage is, from one perspective, the clincher of the prophet's presentation. In many passages thus far, the prophet has proclaimed that God would somehow bring the people out of captivity and into freedom, and would return them to Jerusalem, leading them in a marvelous procession back to the place where they belonged. Now, beginning just a few verses before our reading, the text reveals the instrument that God will use to accomplish this return. The surprising thing is that that instrument is a foreign ruler.

In the past, God may have chosen surprising means to bring about salvation. One thinks of the women in the biblical tradition who were major channels of the people's being saved: Deborah, Hannah, and later Judith and Esther. Even Ruth, the Moabitess, was a surprising choice of instruments, but she was to become the great-grandmother of King David. Balaam, a foreign prophet,

49

would say only good things about Israel. But never before had God chosen a foreign monarch to save the chosen people.

God even addresses Cyrus, king of the Persians, with the title reserved for the descendant of David, the one who would sit on the throne that God had endowed eternally: "anointed" (Hebrew *meshiah,* from which comes our English "Messiah"; Greek *christos,* from which comes our English "Christ"). Here, of course, there is no thought of the Christian idea of the Messiah who saves from sin. Rather, the "anointed" in the Hebrew Bible is always the reigning king who will rule justly. Eventually, the term was applied to the future king who would truly fulfill that role in all its aspects.

The prophet does not stop at calling a foreign ruler by an Israelite title for a king. He continues with ideas and images that belong to the enthronement ceremony in Israel and elsewhere in the ancient Near East. Taking him by the right hand, calling him by name, giving him a name of honor, girding him for battle—all these are part of the enthronement of any king in antiquity. Second Isaiah gives Cyrus all that a deliverer of his people needs to fulfill this special task that God will give him.

The prophet, in his unbounded enthusiasm, lists events that sound like military victories, political advances, and geographical expansion (vv. 1*b*-3). It is not clear how the prophet knew of this foreign king, whom he calls God's "anointed." But the sureness of the prophet on the matter of coming victories is striking. The survey of triumphs continues into the future. "I shall give you treasures from dark vaults." (Some might prefer the older RSV "treasures of darkness.") Who knows what special treasures these might be?

Further benefits promised Cyrus include all sorts of things that will enable him to do the special work assigned him by the God who knows him and calls him. The text suggests that the prophet expected Cyrus to become a worshiper of Yahweh, the God of Israel. Some scholars judge that there is a problem in the text at this point. It is debated whether the prophet expected that Cyrus would acknowledge the God of Israel.

There survives from antiquity the actual inscription on which Cyrus recorded his victories and gave the credit for them to a deity. He credited those victories, not to Yahweh, but to the Babylonian god Marduk. That god, he claimed, took him by the hand and brought him to Marduk's city, so that Cyrus would rule it in justice and righteousness. (One can see the political advantage that this claim would have in some Babylonian circles.) It is clear that an event does not always have the same interpretation for everyone.

The prophet explains the reason for Yahweh's selection and empowerment of Cyrus. It is for the sake of Israel that Yahweh has acted thus. Here Israel gets the title of servant, a title that Cyrus himself does not receive. Israel is in a special relationship to Yahweh, one that will be permanent, while Cyrus, although anointed, has only a temporary role in Yahweh's plan.

The passage closes with another insistence that Yahweh is the only real God in existence. "There is none other." Many people think that this statement is the first full expression of theoretical monotheism in ancient Israel. And for this prophet, the belief in the existence of only one source of all things seems to have suggested that God created all that anyone would ever experience.

An astounding claim occurs only here in all of the Bible: "I make the light, I create the darkness." This certainly is a different view from that in Genesis 1, where God clearly creates only light, while darkness appears as a by-product of this creative action. Blaming God for the bad things that happen to us is a phenomenon still found in our day.

Retelling the Story

Once there was a woman who had a son and a daughter. When the woman fell sick, the entire village grieved for her and prayed for her recovery. The oldest man, grandfather to half of the village, recounted the story of a golden bird whose feathers were rumored to have healing powers. Not only did the feathers bring healing, but anyone who found this bird would be blessed with a treasure as well.

The son was eager to go in search of the bird, hoping for the reward. He envied his younger sister, for although their mother was kind to each of her children, she would often smile when she saw her youngest. So he took the horse and ample provisions and hurried off in the direction of the desert where the fiery bird was rumored to nest. At the end of seven days, the son limped back into the village. When the villagers asked about the horse and his adventure, he would only scowl and declare that fools believed in golden birds and miracles. He was cured of such nonsense now.

The young girl then asked for her mother's blessing and left alone, riding on the back of an ancient mule. She rode steadily for many miles until she came upon a sign. It read, "He who goes right will keep his life but lose his horse. He who goes left will die, but his horse will be spared."

Poor girl. She needed her life and the mule in order to save her mother. "I can't throw my life away before I've made some use out of it. I'm fond of this mule, but I love my mother. Perhaps the danger is only for men who ride horses." And with that thought she went to the right. For two days she rode without seeing a living creature. At sunset on the third day, a great gray wolf blocked her path.

It spoke, "Why have you come this far? Did you not read what was written? All risk will be paid for in suffering." With that, the mule fell dead beneath her, and the wolf disappeared.

The young girl wept over her mule. But when the dawn came she summoned her courage and began walking. She walked for three more days, growing thinner as she walked. At sunset on that day, the wolf reappeared. "Foolish human, why have you come this far? What can you hope to find? All risk will be paid for in suffering." And the great wolf grew larger as the light faded.

"Sir Wolf," said the girl, "I know that I am foolish. I hope to find the golden bird whose feathers bring healing. My mother is ill, and I want her to smile again."

"The feathers take away pain for a season, nothing more," rumbled the wolf. "Your mother will grow older and ill again. There is nothing on earth that will hold back the night of death. Why do you risk such danger to give her just a few days, a few smiles, nothing more? Save your own life."

"But what is life without risk?" asked the young girl. "Are smiles not a treasure? Is home not worth the risk of losing your way?"

The wolf did not answer. It was hard for the girl to see him, for either he had grown so large that he blocked the sky, or the night had grown so dark that all she could see was the fiery gold of the wolf's eyes.

"Come closer, if you dare, little one. Come closer, and I will teach you what treasure is. I will show you well-being and woe. I alone can make the homeless a home." So powerful were the rumbles of the wolf that the girl could feel her chest vibrate, and the golden eyes drew her, step by step.

Closer, closer came the girl to the darkness that had eyes. "Stretch out your hand," rumbled the darkness. "Open your arms." And as the girl, trembling, reached out to touch the night, there was an explosion of fire and golden light. The explosion blinded the girl, and she stumbled, grabbing the black fur as she fell. The ground seemed so far away that she seemed to float, not fall. At last she came to rest. She cautiously opened her eyes to discover that she was in her own home. The girl sprang to her feet and saw in her hand a golden feather. Shouting with joy, she burst into the sickroom and startled the neighbors who were keeping watch over her mother.

When a philosopher told Rabbi Gamaliel that the God of Israel must be a great artist since everything in creation had been made from just so few materials. When the rabbi asked which materials the philosopher meant he said, among others, light and darkness. To which Gamaliel replied by speaking the words of Isaiah, "I (God) make the light, I create the darkness" (Isaiah 45:7) to prove that his God had created everything there is without the help of even those two materials. (*Genesis Rabbah* 1.9 note 5 and *Sefer Ha-Aggadah* 6.5)

"Look, Mother! The golden feather that will take the pain away." But even before she touched her mother with the feather, she saw her mother smile. (*Heather Murray Elkins*)

The Women of Babylon

The queen city, Babylon, will be dishonored and deflowered.

The Story

Come down and sit in the dust,
virgin daughter of Babylon.
Descend from your throne and sit on
  the ground,
daughter of the Chaldaeans;
never again will you be called
tender and delicate.
Take the handmill, grind meal, remove
  your veil;
strip off your skirt, bare your thighs,
  wade through rivers,
so that your nakedness may be seen,
your shame exposed.
I shall take vengeance and show
  clemency to none,
says our Redeemer, the Holy One of
  Israel,
whose name is the LORD of Hosts.
Daughter of the Chaldaeans,
go into the darkness and sit in silence;
for never again will you be called
queen of many kingdoms.
I was angry with my people;
I dishonoured my own possession
and surrendered them into your power.
You showed them no mercy;
even on the aged you laid a very heavy
  yoke.
You said, 'I shall reign a queen for
  ever';
you gave no thought to your actions,
nor did you consider their outcome.
Now listen to this,
you lover of luxury, carefree on your
  throne,

saying to yourself,
'I am, and there is none other.
I shall never sit in widow's mourning,
never know the loss of children.'
Yet suddenly, in a single day,
both these things will come upon you;
they will both come upon you in full
  measure:
loss of children and widowhood,
despite your many sorceries, all your
  countless spells.
Secure in your wicked ways
you thought, 'No one can see me.'
It was your wisdom and knowledge
that led you astray.
You said to yourself,
'I am, and there is none other.'
Therefore evil will overtake you,
and you will not know how to conjure
  it away;
disaster will befall you,
and you will not be able to avert it;
ruin all unforeseen
will suddenly come upon you.
Persist in your spells and your many
  sorceries,
in which you have trafficked all your
  life.
Maybe you can get help from them!
Maybe you will yet inspire terror!

Comments on the Story

The prophet in this passage has a good time at the expense of enemies of God and of God's people. Second Isaiah is convinced that Babylon, the captor of Zion, is going to get deserved punishment. But to say only that the city will fall would be far less fun (and perhaps less convincing) than to say that Babylon, personified as a woman, is really going to lose out in her quest to rule the world. The prophet pulls out all the stops in this depiction of a once great woman.

First, the prophet has God address Babylon with a reverse command. Often in Second Isaiah, God says to Jerusalem, "Arise!" But to Babylon the command is "Come down!" And as if that weren't enough, an additional command is appended, "Sit in the dust!" The verb used here for "to sit" (*yashab*) often means "to rule." The irony is bitter: She who wants to rule the world must sit in the dust. In verse 8, the verb appears again, and this time Babylon will "sit in widow's mourning." The prophet hardly misses a single opportunity to be bitter. The storyteller should not miss the pointed irony.

The feminine dimension of the city goes far back in Canaanite (but not Akkadian) thought. In this passage, Second Isaiah uses the image of the city as a woman in many different ways for Babylon. She is "virgin daughter," words that imply that the city has a filial relation to her god and that she still lives at home, for now, still under that god's protection. She is also the wife (and future widow) of that god. In another way, she is mother of the citizens of the city who worship the city's god.

But now she who was once queen over all the cities of the world (as the prophet chose to see the matter) must give up her throne and her pampered status with all its benefits and all the things one can become attached to. She has to take on the lowly role of a common slave, doing the common chores given them.

Within the context of Second Isaiah, Babylon had lost out to Jerusalem. Jerusalem will now be queen and will receive all that Babylon had desired. For Jerusalem there will be light and brightness. Her children will return to her, coming from far off. Jerusalem, the wife of the true and only God, will take her place as the new Queen of the World. Later on in Second Isaiah (50:1-2), the prophet admits there had been a separation. But that isolation was only temporary.

Babylon, in the meantime, will have all her glory removed. Even her clothes will come off. One may wish that Second Isaiah would have stopped there. "Exposing of nakedness of" refers to sexual intercourse. Here the reference is surely to rape. This prophet, like Hosea, Jeremiah, and especially Ezekiel, takes the image of the city as a woman to perhaps offensive extremes. The rape of a city is an expression that in history all too often became a reality for its female inhabitants. This prophet, however, limits the violation to only the city itself.

The text as its stands (some commentators have suggested that v. 6 is an addition from a later writer) indicates that the people (Israel) had been entrusted to Jerusalem for care. But Jerusalem treated them abusively, even laying "a very heavy yoke" on the aged, an injustice that the societies of the ancient Near East in general would not countenance. This relationship differs from that proposed in Jeremiah 31:22. (One should prefer the NRSV, "a woman encompasses [embraces] a man," to the REB, "a woman will play a man's part.") There the relationship is between a mother and a son: She embraces the son whom she cherishes.

The worst offense that the prophet sees in Babylon is making the claim that Yahweh had made earlier in this section of Isaiah. Yahweh says, "There is none beside me." To hear this on the lips of Babylon has provoked the prophet and leads him to disparage and disgrace this arrogant city. Babylon will become both a childless mother and a husbandless wife. The storyteller might consider the severity of that prediction. Being a wife and mother were then the very things that gave a woman status. All these will not be taken from Babylon.

A charmingly snide remark is made to Babylon in verse 8. She is addressed as "you lover of luxury." (The NKJV renders it "O pampered one.") The word *pampered* comes from the same root as the name of the primordial garden, Eden. Babylon had been a kind of Eden. In 51:3, Zion, the rival of Babylon, will have her wilderness turned "into an Eden." Once again, Babylon does not have a chance against Jerusalem and her God.

The final picture of this city-woman shows her no longer claiming divinity. Rather, she is casting about, looking for something to trust or to hope in— something to avert the disaster that the prophet proclaims will be unavoidable and complete.

Poor Babylon is seen, perhaps, playing her fortune cards, consulting her horoscope, maybe trying whatever lottery was around then. The prophet, though, knows that the city that defied God cannot escape inevitable downfall and punishment.

Retelling the Story

There's a lone grave in a certain southern county near the sea. It's off the main road, and the trees have grown all around, but the grave itself is clearly marked. The small white stone reads simply, "A beloved Teacher." Although the grave is said to be more than a hundred years old, it looks as clean and neat as if the stone had just been set.

Folks in the area say that it's the resting place of a schoolteacher who had taught the children of the early owners of the nearby plantation. They had wanted the best education for their children, so they had sent for a teacher who could teach anything to anybody. And in no time at all, she'd worked a miracle in that place. Johnny could read. Sally could write. And all was well, until this teacher decided to let a few black children come in after school so she might teach them to read and write. Now, the owners didn't like this at all, but they put up with it for a while, since they were so proud of how smart their children had become. But the word began to spread that the brightest child of all was a young black boy who came to school straight from the fields.

> Certain rabbis saw a veiled message in Isaiah's call to the "Virgin daughter of Babylon." What he was really saying, they suggest, was instead, "You think you are young, but you are old. You pretend to be a virgin but you are a whore. Come sit in the dirt where you belong." (*Song of Songs Rabbah* 3.4 [2])

When a large number of slaves escaped to freedom, the owners decided that the lessons would have to stop. So they torched the houses of the slaves who seemed too bold, too proud. The young bright boy was killed in the fire. The schoolteacher grieved and grieved, but the classes for black children stopped.

Several months after the fire, a prideful boy whose father owned the biggest plantation was disciplined by the teacher for something cruel he had done. As he passed by the schoolhouse at the end of the day, he saw the teacher talking to a small black cat. He headed home and told his parents about this teacher who talked to black cats. He insisted that she'd called the cat by the name of the young boy who had died in the fire. Now that he thought about it, he told them, this teacher used to do other strange things. He was sure he'd heard her mutter words in Latin or some other "incantation" right out loud in the schoolroom. His parents told other parents, and fear and superstition did the rest. A mob gathered outside her house, and when she walked out to try to calm them, she was killed on the spot.

> The "you" in verse 6 into whose hand God surrendered the people was Rome, according to the rabbis living under Roman rule. Rome is described as a swine, the worst animal that could represent a nation. Rome is piggish because its citizens do not treat strangers in their midst with the hospitality due them. (*Leviticus Rabbah* 13.5)

When morning came, reason returned, and several of the women went to tend the body, while her coffin was built by one of the slaves. They picked a place for the grave that was not on "holy ground," and where the stone came from, no one knew or would say.

In time, the school was reopened, but the new teacher came from the county seat and neither used any kind of foreign language nor practiced strange ways. If it wasn't in the book, it wasn't taught, and nobody who wasn't white was taught to read. But the strangest thing happened in that school. No matter how hard the teacher worked or how long the children studied, they seemed to get duller by the day. Sally had trouble making her letters, and Johnny stumbled when he read aloud. Some folks began to whisper that the school had been cursed. So they tore it down and built a new one near the center of town. But no child ever amounted to much from that place. One or two families tried sending their sons away to fancy schools in the East. But the ones who went never came back, and after the war the entire community seemed to come undone and drift away. But if you ever travel through that part of the country, go and visit the single grave within a circle of trees. The grave is neat, and the stone looks like it was set just yesterday. *(Heather Murray Elkins)*

Second Servant Song

The servant will suffer exhaustion and opposition, but will win glory for God. As a reward, he will become a light to all peoples.

The Story

Listen to me, you coasts and
islands,
pay heed, you peoples far distant:
the LORD called me before I was born,
he named me from my mother's
womb.
He made my tongue a sharp sword
and hid me under the shelter of his
hand;
he made me into a polished arrow,
in his quiver he concealed me.
He said to me, 'Israel, you are my
servant
through whom I shall win glory.'
Once I said, 'I have toiled in vain;
I have spent my strength for nothing,
and to no purpose.'
Yet my cause is with the LORD
and my reward with my God.
The LORD had formed me in the womb
to be his servant,
to bring Jacob back to him
that Israel should be gathered to him,
so that I might rise to honour in the
LORD's sight
and my God might be my strength.
And now the LORD has said to me:
'It is too slight a task for you, as my
servant,
to restore the tribes of Jacob,
to bring back the survivors of Israel:
I shall appoint you a light to the
nations
so that my salvation may reach earth's

farthest bounds.'
These are the words of the Holy One,
the LORD who redeems Israel,
to one who is despised,
and whom people abhor,
the slave of tyrants:
Kings will rise when they see you,
princes will do homage,
because of the LORD who is faithful,
because of Israel's Holy One who has
chosen you.
These are the words of the LORD:
In the time of my favour I answered
you;
on the day of deliverance I came to
your aid.
I have formed you, and destined you
to be a light for peoples,
restoring the land
and allotting once more its desolate
holdings.
I said to the prisoners, 'Go free,'
and to those in darkness, 'Come out
into the open.'
Along every path they will find pasture
and grazing in all the arid places.
They will neither hunger nor thirst,
nor will scorching heat or sun distress
them;
for one who loves them will guide
them
and lead them by springs of water.
I shall make every hill a path
and raise up my highways.

They are coming: some from far away,
some from the north and the west,
and others from the land of Syene.
Shout for joy, you heavens; earth,
 rejoice;
break into songs of triumph, you
 mountains,
for the LORD has comforted his people
and has had pity on them in their
 distress.
But Zion says,
'The LORD has forsaken me;
my LORD has forgotten me.'
Can a woman forget the infant at her
 breast,
or a mother the child of her womb?
But should even these forget,

I shall never forget you.
I have inscribed you on the palms of
 my hands;
your walls are always before my eyes.
Those who rebuild you make better
 speed
than those who pulled you down,
while those who laid you waste leave
 you and go.
Raise your eyes and look around:
they are all assembling, flocking back
 to you.
By my life I, the LORD, swear it:
you will wear them as your jewels,
and adorn yourself with them like a
 bride.

Comments on the Story

This reading begins with the section known as the second Servant Song (49:1-6). In the previous song (Isa. 42:1-4), God spoke about the Servant, and in the verses that follow (42:5-7) God continues to speak directly to the Servant about the mission he receives.

In the present song the servant speaks for himself about himself and the task he has been given. That task looms large and demanding. A new dimension is given to it as well. Now the task will clearly take a toll on the servant, and he will be caused to suffer exhaustion and opposition in the very work that he has been assigned—indeed, the work for which he was born.

The Servant's appeal to the distant coasts and peoples is a majestic opening. Indeed, the call to nations emphasizes the international and universal scope that this prophet has. But the appeal also echoes the desire for the God of Israel to be known as the one true God, over and against the gods of the Babylonians.

The Servant starts by giving his own credentials: He was called before birth. He says that, while still in his mother's womb, Yahweh gave him the calling about which he must now speak. He will speak of his role and the experience he already has had in the very exercise of that role.

The images the prophet uses for his self-description come from the realm of the military and from the world of archery, whether for hunting or for battle. The choice of specific images enhances the idea that the role of the Servant involves words. Words and their message should shoot out from the Servant and into the hearts of those who are listening. The Servant is clearly called to speak. Will he find listeners?

The Servant quotes what God had said to him, at some earlier time to which the readers had not yet been privy. "Israel, you are my servant/ through whom I shall win glory." The claim that God will "win glory" through the Servant is rather extraordinary. One usually thinks of God's being able to get glory independently of human help. This time God ties the divine glory to the work of a human being, the Servant.

Verse 3 is the only place in the four songs where the Servant seems to be named. He is called "Israel." Moreover, two verses later, the Servant, surprisingly, has a mission to Israel, to "gather," "bring back," "restore" Israel. This would require two Israels, each different from the other. (Is the Servant the "ideal" Israel?) One Greek manuscript of Isaiah does not have the word *Israel* in this verse. Indeed, the verse seems, to some interpreters, overloaded with words. These observations are some of the reasons why certain scholars think that this word is an addition to the text by a scribe at a time later than that of our prophet. If this word is an addition to the text here (which seems likely), then the scribe who made the addition would have been the first person to give the Servant a collective interpretation (instead of the individual servant who would restore Israel).

The Servant, in verse 4, gives an assessment of his work thus far. It has been exhausting and futile. His work has brought no success in the normal sense of the word. Tired and dejected as he is, the Servant still feels that God is on his side. Spent and worn, the servant is convinced that God will repay his devotion to his task.

A major development takes place. The task of the Servant thus far had been "to bring Jacob back," to "gather" Israel to God. Now the calling of the Servant is expanded beyond the boundaries of his own people. "A light to the nations/ so that my salvation may reach earth's farthest bounds" is indeed no small idea, no trifling matter. On hearing these words, the Servant must have stood in awe of such a call. Who could simply say "Okay" without a sea of questions and an ocean of doubts?

The usual end of this "song" is verse 6. The next verses, nevertheless, could be taken as if they were being addressed to the same person. The problem is that the person addressed in verse 8 has already experienced some kind of salvation. God had already come to his aid, and he has received favor. This person, however, is given the same title that is given in 42:6, "a light for peoples." (The comments on that passage mention the difference between the REB and the RSV on this phrase.) This recurrence of the phrase shows a continuity among the Servant songs and an affinity with the rest of the texts, among which the songs occur.

Verse 7 has many of the phrases that link the songs to the whole segment of Isaiah 40–55 and to the book as a whole. The expression "the Holy One of Israel" and the very idea of the holiness of God are two ideas that recur in the three parts of the book (chaps. 1–39; 40–55; 56–66). Another attractive aspect of the book and this segment of it is the appearance of kings (v. 7) who will acknowledge the addressee and the work of his God.

God takes the lead in the announcement of salvation and deliverance to come. Imagery of God as shepherd, which has already occurred, recurs here (vv. 9-12). And it is now God who makes the highway for the people to return to the holy city. Not surprisingly, all creation bursts into songs of praise (v. 13) for the redeeming work of God toward the exiles as they, in vision, are led back.

The last five verses of this passage introduce the character Zion, who dominates the second half of the section (chaps. 49–55). Zion is the religious name for Jerusalem, the city of God. It is to that city that God will lead back the exiles. Zion herself speaks. Her first speech is short, a statement of abandonment by God.

God's response to Zion, the first time she is addressed in Isaiah 40–55, is a moving insistence that God could never simply give her up. Strikingly, the divine speech compares God to a mother (perhaps the prophet was thinking of Zion's motherhood). The intimacy between God and the city is like that between a person and his or her own body.

God reassures Zion not only that she will be rebuilt, but also that she will see the return of all her children who had been sent away. God is so moved on this occasion that God instinctively thinks of Zion as a bride, God's own.

Retelling the Story

The cemetery once was guarded by a high stone wall, and the gate was narrow and straight. Now the stones have lost their posture and spill right and left of their place, letting anyone step over. The gate remains open, half off its hinges, like a watchman asleep at his post. Perhaps once or twice a decade, a social climber of family trees wanders among the headstones, looking for familiar names. A young soldier of the Civil War is supposed to rest in peace within this hallowed ground, but his actual whereabouts are unknown, so even Veterans' Day passes without comment. Edged up against a hill in West-by-God Virginia, the main road directs attention and traffic away from its gate, but the laughter and odor of the nearby Dairy Dip drift up the hills to keep company with those who try to rest in peace.

If you work your way to the shady side where the tall maples have provided layers of warmth with their leaves, a family plot unfolds. The first marker is a small, nameless stone, the writing long eroded. The second marker is small, but the words have survived the weather: "Our rose has bloomed in heaven." The third marker is small as well: "Home with God." The fourth marker bears a name, "Robert—age 8 yrs. 2 mnths." The fifth marker is adult sized, and here, the climax of the family plot is revealed: "Rachel, whose children are no more." There is no sign of the author of those stony lines. Perhaps he wandered off to rest in peace beside another who bore his name and children in a happier frame. Perhaps he is the spirit of the gate, hanging on and open for the One who comes to console Jerusalem.

If you follow the north wall, stepping over the fallen river stones that no one now has the skill to stack, you will stumble on a half-buried marker that promises treasure. It lures visitors like a Rosetta Stone, hinting at the code that will crack this stony silence into speech. This stone is larger than all the other markers. The quality of marble is finer than its neighbors, and the upper half of the stone bears a finely etched wreath of olives. Beneath the wreath, the tribute is carved in a heavy hand: "To the Eternal Memory of . . . "

The appeal of a hero's story leads one to kneel and work at clearing the name of the person who deserves more than this forgotten end. The stone has sunk, covering the name of the person whom others wanted to be known and remembered. So you pull at the grass until the lower half can be read again, resurrecting human accomplishment and pride. "To the Eternal Memory of . . . " and the name is missing. "Who . . . " and whatever whoever had done has been erased. "And died in . . . " and even the date of this person's departure is now known only to God.

The wind seems colder now, the Dairy Dip's laughter more mocking as it rises with the smell of greasy french fries. So you wipe your hands and decide it's time to visit one of the more permanent monuments to human pride—a shopping mall. But

If anyone studies Torah and is honest in business and compassionate in dealing with others, people say of that person's teachers that they are blessed. Just so Isaiah says "Israel, you are my servant through whom I shall win glory" (49:3). God, the giver of the Torah is glorified and blessed by the behavior of those who study and follow the divine way laid out therein. On the other hand, if someone studies Torah and is dishonest in business and lacking in compassion, people say of that person's teachers that they are to be pitied. (*Sefer Ha-Aggadah* 434.306)

When the prophet says, "my reward (is) with my God," the sages compared this to a king who had prepared a feast for his friends. He called for them to come the day before the feast and took them into the banquet hall. There the king described in intimate detail the look and taste and smell of every dish that was to be served. The guests imagined what a delight the meal would be and slept at ease that night awaiting it. Just so the righteous sleep at ease, for they know the reward that God has prepared for them. (*Sefer Ha-Aggadah* 292.491)

as you are making your way along the wall, a scrawl catches your eyes, emerging like the fiery letters on Nebuchanezzar's wall. Written by some unknown hand, the truth survives, graffiti-form. "God knows . . . " And suddenly you have a vision of the gate, lifted up and swinging open. You hold your breath for a second and wonder who's coming. *(Heather Murray Elkins)*

Third Servant Song

The Servant will suffer from physical torture and insults, but not from guilt.

The Story

The Lord GOD has given me the tongue of one who has been instructed
to console the weary
with a timely word;
he made my hearing sharp every morning,
that I might listen like one under instruction.
The Lord GOD opened my ears
and I did not disobey or turn back in defiance.
I offered my back to the lash,
and let my beard be plucked from my chin,
I did not hide my face from insult and spitting.

But the Lord GOD is my helper;
therefore no insult can wound me;
I know that I shall not be put to shame,
therefore I have set my face like flint.
One who will clear my name is at my side.
Who dare argue against me? Let us confront one another.
Who will dispute my cause? Let him come forward.
The Lord GOD is my helper;
who then can declare me guilty?

Comments on the Story

This reading is known among modern Bible readers as the third of the four Songs of the Servant of the Lord. In the second song (49:1-6), the Servant spoke of his exhaustion and despondency at his people's lack of a proper response to his preaching. This current song brings forward new ideas about the role of the Servant and helps storytellers to address the idea of the suffering that has become part of the Servant's life. Moreover, in this song, the Servant becomes more explicit about several things: his calling, his relationship with God, and the different kinds of suffering he has had to endure. The passage presents more ideas on the gifts and functions of this mysterious figure.

The intimacy between God and the Servant is especially evident in this song. God is his teacher, his healer, his helper, and his defender. The Servant is empowered to accomplish his task and to endure the suffering involved in it.

Focus falls initially on facial aspects of the Servant: tongue, ears, beard. Not surprisingly, the tongue is mentioned first because it is the prophet's means of expression. The spoken word is the ordinary way prophets communicate with their people. The Servant claims special training from God for this important role.

The Servant's first specific use of speech reveals much about his role: He is to console the weary. The concern that God has for the weak is embodied in the concern for his fellow suffering humans that God commands the Servant to have. The "weary" here refers to the exiles themselves, and their rejection of the Servant is all the more disheartening because of his own graciousness.

Emphasis is also given to the sense of hearing. God sharpens the Servant's ability in this matter. God even "opens the ear" of the Servant. In striking imagery, God is the one who not only speaks but also enables the Servant to truly hear the divine word. The reader is assured that God can do all. One never need wonder whether God can accomplish what is wanted and what is needed. For all practical purposes, the Servant sees that when God participates in an enterprise, that effort will succeed.

The Servant is personally instructed by God for this task. Each day God attends to the Servant so that he can better execute the assignment given him. And the response of the Servant is admirable and is a model for all who would respond to God. The Servant listens well and does not "turn his back" (or in contemporary idiom, "burn out") on the suffering his work demands.

This continual devotion of the Servant to his task is all the more admirable to storytellers, for it entails suffering to a frightening degree. The kind of punishment described by the "lash" and the "plucking" is not actually clear. Some commentators have suggested that these details are exaggerated speech for the contempt shown by the servant's audience when he spoke publicly. In verse 6, the word "insult" agrees with the proposal that the physical imagery is symbolic. But the next word, "spitting," again leaves open the possibility that the servant did suffer physically in his work.

In an almost uncanny way, the Servant is convinced of the presence of the one "who vindicates me" (NRSV) or "who will clear my name" (REB). God has not given the Servant an impossible task. Neither has God given the task and gone off somewhere. God remains with the Servant through it all. The Servant is fully convinced that nothing can thwart the work that God has given him. No challenge or challenger will be able to confront the Servant and win.

The prophet/Servant is using the strongest language that this individual knows. There is the overwhelming desire to convince the hearers or readers that God is protector, defender, and ultimately judge. For this purpose, language from the law court is employed. A summons to the court proceedings can be found in Isaiah 41:1, and one hears echoes of the presentation of the case in Isaiah 41:21-23. It is interesting that this prophet seems to employ this legal setting and vocabulary when it is most desirous to convince (e.g., Isa. 41:1-5, 21-29; 43:8-15).

Is the Servant's conviction that his work will be victorious well founded? Will his trust in God and the divine protection really prove true? The last of the Servant Songs (Isa. 52:13–53:12) will answer these questions.

Retelling the Story

The young teacher had walked a long way that day, and the sun was touching the trees when the house came in sight. He shifted his bag from his sore shoulder to his tired hand and knocked at the narrow door. As he waited for a response, he looked at the porch, the unlit windows. This would be his home for the next few years. He hoped the gray, stingy look to the place was due to the fading light, but the melt-down mouth of the man who opened the door added to the gloom.

By the time a sparse supper had been served and put away, the young man's heart was as cold as the hearth. His great adventure of learning was turning into a hard lesson. His grit-eyed employer sat across from him at the table, writing down the terms of his contract. Slave wages he'd expected. Teaching was seen as a sorry trade, a man's man could do better. Twenty-five dollars a month and a place to board was generally considered plenty for "book larnin'." But he hadn't calculated on Mr. Tuggle, chairman of the school board and ruling elder of this part of creation. For the privilege of Mr. Tuggle's enforced hospitality of a meager breakfast and supper and one corner bed under the eaves, Harold had to pay twenty dollars a month. Since Mr. Tuggle was also the treasurer, that meant he would receive five dollars, and not a penny more, every thirty days for two years. Too tired to do more than sigh and sign away his life, Harold stretched out on the thin ticking covered mattress, and fell asleep.

The biscuits were hard, the coffee bitter, and the morning too cold and early. But under his polite ways and quiet voice, Harold's mind was rumbling with the force of an engine. Once he saw the children and heard their hunger for what they couldn't even articulate or for things they could not name, he was truly caught. He would stay, not turn on his heels and shake off their dust. But what to do about old Mr. Tuggle?

Before Isaiah accepted the assignment to be God's prophet he was warned that the people to whom he would speak could be hardheaded and unwilling to listen. He was told that he and his words would not be received gladly in many places. In response, the sages say, Isaiah told God, "I will offer my back to the lash, and let my beard be plucked out from my chin. I will not hide my face from insult and spitting." Perhaps this could be the oath of office for a prophet ancient or modern. (*Leviticus Rabbah* 10.2)

By the end of two weeks, several of the children's parents had warmed enough to him to take pity on him and offer him other lodging for less than half of Tuggle's rate. Harold smiled all the way home, along the valley and across the swinging bridge that spanned the creek next to Tuggle's sparse house. But between the porch and the door, the smile traded places. The old man was ready. Rumors of the valley's unexpected hospitality had already reached him. Sure, Harold could pack his bag and move on; this was a free country. The only trouble was, and here the old man grinned like a fox, the bridge belonged to him.

Now, Harold could lodge with somebody else. But the families who had offered him rooms were on this side of the fast creek, which was really a small river. The school house lay across the creek. No bridge meant a four-mile walk up the mountains until the source of the water narrowed enough for a crossing. There was only one place close by that the water narrowed and could be crossed, and Tuggle's bridge was built right on that spot. If the young, snot-nosed city boy touched that bridge, old Tuggle would teach him what private property meant.

Every morning for a month, Harold would rise before dawn and make his way along the path that led beside the bridge and up the mountain. And every morning, Tuggle was waiting with a shotgun across his knees, grinning like a fox. Every evening, as he made his weary way down the mountain, Tuggle stood guard on his porch. But one morning after a month of tramping up and down the mountain, Harold strolled toward the bridge and stopped. The old man stood, shouting curses as he cocked the gun. But Harold simply balanced two strong saplings, one in either hand, and stepped up to slip his feet into the straps. Right under Tuggle's red nose, Harold waded on homemade stilts across the narrowest part of the creek, right beside the bridge Tuggle had built.

Of course, that battle was won by Harold, but Tuggle didn't give up the war for two years and ten months. Every morning and evening he sat, dangerously silent with his gun ready, growing grimmer and grayer each day. At the end of his contract with the school, Harold wanted to let Tuggle know that he harbored no ill feelings toward him. He paid the postman extra to deliver those stilts right to Tuggle's porch. And valley folk say that they found Tuggle the next morning, dead in his chair, with a death grip on those saplings. That shows you what a little learning can amount to. *(Heather Murray Elkins)*

Paradise Regained

To those who have no hope, the prophet describes new beginnings.

The Story

Listen to me,
all who follow after the right, who
seek the LORD:
consider the rock from which you were
hewn,
the quarry from which you were cut;
consider Abraham your father
and Sarah who gave you birth:
when I called him he was but one;
I blessed him and made him many.
The LORD has comforted Zion,
comforted all her ruined homes,
turning her wilderness into an Eden,
her arid plains into a garden of the
LORD.
Gladness and joy will be found in her,
thanksgiving and melody.
Pay heed to me, my people,
and listen to me, my nation,
for instruction will shine forth from me
and my judgment will be a light to
peoples.
In an instant I bring near my victory;
my deliverance will appear
and my arm will rule the peoples;
coasts and islands will wait for me
and look to me for protection.
Raise your eyes heavenwards;
look on the earth beneath:
though the heavens be dispersed as
smoke
and the earth wear out like a garment
and its inhabitants die like flies,
my deliverance will be everlasting
and my saving power will remain
unbroken.

Comments on the Story

In this passage, Second Isaiah continues his attempt to convince those who hear or read his words that God will surely deliver the exiles and bring them back to Zion. The prophet has already tried various tacks to catch their attention, to present the possibility, and to assure the people that God will surely act.

The address to "all who follow the right" or "all who pursue justice" (NKJV) might be a ploy to win the favor of the audience. But those "who seek the Lord" are clearly more specific. Salvation will come for those who expect and wait for it. The phrase "seek the Lord" in preexilic times referred to those going to the local religious place of worship and sacrifice. For those in exile, however, the phrase is freed from the physical aspects it once had.

The reference to "rock" and "quarry" is quite surprising. Some commentators have referred to an ancient myth (and some more recent folk tales) according to which humanity actually came from such material. The reference could hardly be to God as a physical source, for the Bible never says that human beings physically came out of God. Rather, the reference is to Abraham and Sarah.

It might seem surprising that the seven passages that mention Abraham in the prophetic books all seem to date from exilic or postexilic times. Second Isaiah decides to use this tradition of the ancestral couple, regardless of how old or recent it might be, because his strong desire to convince others allows him to use everything that makes for assurance. Abraham, as the one who received not just a promise, but the honor of being the start of a new age, is certainly a marvelous figure for the prophet to invoke. It is, indeed, a faithful God of whom the prophet speaks.

Any woman will probably rejoice that Sarah is mentioned along with Abraham. This prophet alone recalls Abraham's wife, and it is no surprise that she is mentioned only once and never again. Once noticed, she disappears, but her husband continues in the light. Social historians have different assessments of the exile and its influence for the status of women within the biblical community. A significant number of commentators think that the exclusion of women from temple worship begins at the time of the postexile temple.

The emphasis in this passage here falls directly on the power of God. In the past, God took one man and from him made a whole people, giving that person and that people a powerful blessing. That same God can do things just as tremendous in any age.

The prophet reaches still further for convincing images. The garden in which God put the first human pair, Eden, is the place of beginning and of carefree enjoyment. Zion's wilderness and deserted places will become Eden. Yahweh *comforts* Zion—the very word that Second Isaiah began with: "Comfort, bring comfort to my people." Again we encounter the phenomenon that what Yahweh had told others to do, now Yahweh does. The storyteller might see drama in God's doing what others had been told to do.

The holy city is going to become the place for true joy and unbounded rejoicing. All sorrow and insufficiency will end. Zion, the chosen dwelling place of God, is the one source for happiness and gladness.

In a clever twist, Yahweh briefly is in the place of Zion. The text says that "instruction" will go forth from Yahweh. Second Isaiah claims that Zion will be the place from which emanates instruction. This identification of Yahweh and the city is effective. And the parallel between God and others is emphasized and recast by the statement that Yahweh's judgment itself will be a "light to peoples" (v. 4), the very phrase that described the Servant.

The nearness of God's deliverance is important for the prophet. The prophet claims that the people need not wait a long time for this deliverance to occur. (Their exile must already have seemed a long time for the Jews in Babylon.)

The victory, the judgment of God, is coming soon, the prophet says. Even the people should be aware. The deliverance will be "everlasting," and God's saving power will be "unbroken."

Whether giving a dramatic gesture or simply using a stock phrase, the prophet points to the whole expanse of the universe as it was then known, as speakers for God sang in effect, "All this could crumble, but my coming salvation can't be budged." The prophet proclaims the divine action as the security for all who receive it as their own.

What an astounding claim for a displaced person to make! This prophet is a person whose God lost a war and whose name posterity did not record. Perhaps we can learn much about confident trust from this prophetic conviction.

Retelling the Story

Back in the days of slavery, there was a white family that had always planted corn and did their own work in the fields. When they noticed that all their neighbors made more money planting cotton, they started to plant cotton, too. After a while, they made enough to afford what they needed and then some. "Why should we work from morning to night?" they asked themselves. "Just because our mothers and fathers did doesn't mean we have to." So they bought a few slaves, and then a few more, so they wouldn't have to work at all.

Now they were really free. They bought fancy clothes, built a big fancy house, did whatever they fancied. They liked the way they looked in their new clothes so much that they took down their family pictures, bought big mirrors, and hung them all over the house. They could see their own images in every room, and they looked better than their kin and just as good as their neighbors.

Now, the slaves who worked in the fields didn't have any mirrors. One day a big mirror fell right off the wall while the old farmer was admiring his fancy suit. A broken mirror was bad luck, so he ordered his wife to bury the pieces. She ordered the cook, who ordered the maid, who ordered the head man of the field hands to bury the pieces in the field farthest from the house.

As the head man carried the pieces of the mirror, he looked into one piece and, of course, saw himself. But he didn't know what he was seeing. He'd never seen a mirror. He'd been told that he looked just like his daddy, who had been sold off when he was young. So he thought that it was his daddy he was seeing, that his daddy had come back for his son.

He began talking to his daddy and crying and telling him how hard life

> When the prophet speaks of God comforting all the ruined homes of Zion he is referring to God's role in the rebuilding of the holy city Jerusalem. This was thought of as God's home as well as the home of God's people. (*Exodus Rabbah* 52.5)

was. After a while, the other men and women in the field heard him and gathered around. Sure enough, when they picked up pieces of that mirror, they thought they were seeing their mother or father or some relative they resembled.

After some of the commotion had died down, they each took a piece of the mirror and hid it. The head man dug up the ground so it looked like something was buried, but not one piece of their ancestors went underground.

The sages told a story about a king who had a daughter whom he loved very much. At first he called her his daughter, but after she had grown in both years and wisdom he began to refer to her as his sister. Later, as his love and respect deepened even more he called her his mother. Just so, God calls Israel "sister" in Song of Songs, and some rabbis suggest that in Isaiah the Hebrew word translated "my nation" is really a related word which means "my mother." This simply demonstrates God's deep love and respect for the people. (*Song of Songs Rabbah* 3:11 [2], *Exodus Rabbah* 52.5 and *Numbers Rabbah* 12.8)

Every morning, before they started to work, the field hands would slip away to the place where the mirror pieces were hidden and talk to their ancestors. Sometimes, late at night, when there was only firelight to see by, they would bring all the family together. Together, there by the fire, they would dream and cry and sing. Together with their fathers and mothers, they would remember where they had come from, and no slave ever broke down crazy in that place again. But when the farmer's wife ran off with a neighbor, that old farmer hanged himself, fancy suit and all. Broken mirrors bring bad luck for some. *(Heather Murray Elkins)*

ISAIAH 52:7-10

The Once and Future City of God

The liberation of Jerusalem is so certain that time is no constraint.

The Story

How beautiful on the mountains are
   the feet of the herald,
the bringer of good news,
announcing deliverance,
proclaiming to Zion, 'Your God has
   become king.'
Your watchmen raise their voices
and shout together in joy;
for with their own eyes they see
the LORD return to Zion.

Break forth together into shouts of joy,
you ruins of Jerusalem;
for the LORD has comforted his
   people,
he has redeemed Jerusalem.
The LORD has bared his holy arm
in the sight of all nations,
and the whole world from end to end
shall see the deliverance wrought by
   our God.

Comments on the Story

This is a choice passage in Second Isaiah where there is a virtual summary of the prophet's teaching. The reader should not be distracted by a small phrase in the opening. The "beauty of the feet" should not be a focus of attention. Rather, the message of the one who comes to announce deliverance is the joyous theme. And the prophet can hardly maintain composure in the telling.

The prophet does not shout "Victory!" as the first words of the speech. He cries, "Your God has become king." This cry is almost identical to the opening of several psalms (e.g., Psalms 93; 97; 99). This exclamation begins the praise of God as creator. Indeed, biblically God becomes king by the act of creation. This view of a god and creation is standard both in Mesopotamia and in ancient Israel. The prophet's comparison of the coming deliverance to a new creation leads to this proclamation of God as king. As such, the proclamation of this event is tremendously good news.

The conviction of the prophet is so strong that this future act of liberation and deliberation is told mostly as if it were already past. The storyteller has an opportunity for a similar twist in a retelling. The foretelling of past events is much easier than the prediction of future events as if they were past. On the other hand, perhaps, in moments of intense excitement ideas of time and sequence do not matter at all.

Practicalities are not taken into account in this passage. The watchmen pre-

73

sumably do their watching from the walls. But verse 9 addresses not the walls, but only the ruins. Both watchmen and ruins join in the shouts of exaltation. The watchmen see ("eye by eye," the Hebrew might be read) the Lord return to his beloved city.

"The LORD has comforted his people." Again God does what others had been asked to do. "The redemption of Jerusalem" uses the word (and perhaps the idea) of an unmarried man who is marrying his sister-in-law when her husband (his brother) has died. God has stepped in to take care of those in desperate need.

The "baring of the arm" before the whole world might appear to some readers as a bit odd. It is not exactly rolling up one's sleeves for work. And it is less likely any kind of showing of skin for its own sake. Rather, the image is that of a warrior who takes his sword from within the folds of his garment. The image can be seen in Psalm 74:11, where the psalmist asks God: "Why do you hold back your hand, / why keep your right hand within your bosom?" For the prophet, God now does not hold back.

The prophet announces that the whole world will see the deliverance that the God of Israel is working for the city and its people. It is remarkable that this prophet, living among the relatively small group of Jewish exiles who shared the experience of exile with many other groups of people whom the Babylonian Empire had displaced, would see the whole world watching the Jewish group be saved. If the prophet had really thought about this idea, there might not have been such an unhesitating and comprehensive claim that everyone on earth would see this event.

But if one wants to be empathetic with the prophet, one must appreciate the fact that this prophet brought the special message that unmerited forgiveness was available and that an act of gracious deliverance would come through the most unlikely of means: a foreign ruler.

The joy, the enthusiasm, the conviction, and the hard-hitting attempt to convince—all should be understood in this special setting of exile. This prophet plumbed the depths of literary resources in order to convey the message of salvation coming from God.

Retelling the Story

If you really want to know when the bad got better in this part of the woods, ask Miss Bess. She'll tell you it all started when old man Maxwell died without a will. That was the beginning, but it wasn't clear that *good* was the word for it. Things looked pretty dim, even to Miss Bess, who was born and reared in this place, and insists she wouldn't trade it for any place else 'cept heaven.

She knew this county seat when there were farmers' heavy wagons rumbling around the square, and high-stepping horses and shays hitched beside the court-

74

house steps. She remembers when the Baptists and Methodists and even the Presbyterians had a full house on Sunday morning, and you couldn't go very far off Main Street before you heard six or seven holiness crowds making a joyful noise. Those were the days when town and country rubbed elbows at the bank or George's store and the editor of the *Journal* had to pick out which piece of news to use.

Miss Bess held the keys to the town library as well as the Historical Society's pride and joy, the Bee Hotel/Museum, so she knows when things began to slow down, and then unravel. She has always had a sharp nose for news, both local and larger.

The depression hit hard, but so did the war. Men who marched off for Europe and then for Korea didn't come marching home to stay. They drifted about for a bit after the parades were over, but somehow there wasn't much work to be found.

A person could always eat if he farmed, but crops just didn't seem to pay for shoes, new ovens, or owning a new car. All this craze for cars looked good at first. There was oil and gas tucked under nearly every inch of the county. That's where old man Maxwell got his grip on the future: he traveled up and down the farms, signing oil and gas leases. Folks who hoped to hold on to their land took the lease money and waited for the big oil companies to strike oil in their backyards. The wells were drilled, but sealed, and after a while, even lease money looked like a gamble.

Nobody left the land willingly. It was like pulling up stumps, but after a while the land that was leased was sold. Nobody seemed to have much credit at the bank, 'cept for old man Maxwell. He ended up holding the deeds to half the county. When the country folks moved on, the town folks had to follow, so he ended up buying many of the town's buildings as well. Things slowed to a crawl; the courtyard steps had crabgrass in the cracks. The Main Street churches held on to their firm foundations, but the congregations shrunk down to a few pews and only the Nazarenes could be heard praising God on Sunday morning.

The politicians stopped coming by, but sent their campaign posters to be mounted around the courthouse and in the empty storefront windows. The posters went up, but nobody ever

The sages noted that both masculine and feminine forms are used in various passages to portray God's speaking to the people. They noticed, for example, that the "good news" in Isaiah 52 is masculine in Hebrew while the "good news" in Isaiah 40 is feminine. While they do not seem to make the leap beyond grammatical gender, we might surmise that these could include speech from God that indicates both a masculine and a feminine aspect. (*Ecclesiastes Rabbah* 7.27 [1])

seemed to take them down, so the same names and faces weathered the changes of time. It might have been those posters that put that moneymaking idea in old man Maxwell's head. If it hadn't been for Miss Bess and her habit of reading out-of-town newspapers, nobody would have known about Maxwell's scheme to turn the county into a trash heap. It seems as if some politicians were looking for a place to dump toxic waste, and old man Maxwell was ready to sign away his land.

For someone so quiet, Miss Bess could stir up a storm. She went family to family, told the story, and called a meeting. She gathered everybody in the school gym that had been closed for repairs, and talked about the future. Of course, old man Maxwell tried to make it sound like he was providing jobs for people, but who wants to make a living from storing poison? He was voted down, and that must have upset him so much that he went home and died that very night.

Since there wasn't a will, things were pretty confusing. The state wanted its money, but the town's lawyers had worked it out so that all of old man Maxwell's property could not be divided and then sold. Any buyer would have to buy the whole thing, all or nothing. Who wanted to buy half a county and half a county seat? The folks who were left were shaking their heads and planning to pack up since there wasn't much to hope for. Then the Nazarene preacher heard about this entire community of religious folks who were looking for a new home. Seems as if they were being crowded out and wanted a place that was off the main road of modern life.

The mayor got word to them, and some of the folks came for a visit. They dressed in dark clothes, talked like the King James Bible, and we hear they have lots of kids and are very good farmers. They bought all of old man Maxwell's land, even the empty stores. It seems as if everybody is curious about how they will live once they arrive. They told Miss Bess and the Mayor that tourists will start showing up. The new owners will rent the stores to local folks who want to set up shop and sell handmade things to the tourists. There's even talk about reopening the old hotel as a bed-and-breakfast, but for now, everybody's standing on one foot, waiting for these folks to arrive. Miss Bess doesn't know if they'll come in trucks, or drive all the way here in their wagons. Even the slightest sound sends folks to their windows. It's a happy, nervous sort of waiting, listening for the future. *(Michael E. Williams)*

Fourth Servant Song

Although they despise and slaughter the disfigured Servant, he bears their pain and guilt.

The Story

B ut you will not come out in urgent
    haste
or leave like fugitives;
for the LORD will go before you,
your rearguard will be Israel's God.
My servant will achieve success,
he will be raised to honour, high and
    exalted.
Time was when many were appalled at
    you, my people;
so now many nations recoil at the
    sight of him,
and kings curl their lips in disgust.
His form, disfigured, lost all human
    likeness;
his appearance so changed he no
    longer looked like a man.
They see what they had never been
    told
and their minds are full of things
    unheard before.
Who could have believed what we
    have heard?
To whom has the power of the LORD
    been revealed?
He grew up before the LORD like a
    young plant
whose roots are in parched ground;
he had no beauty, no majesty to catch
    our eyes,
no grace to attract us to him.
He was despised, shunned by all,
pain-racked and afflicted by disease;
we despised him, we held him of no
    account,

an object from which people turn away
    their eyes.
Yet it was our afflictions he was
    bearing,
our pain he endured,
while we thought of him as smitten by
    God,
struck down by disease and misery.
But he was pierced for our
    transgressions,
crushed for our iniquities;
the chastisement he bore restored us
    to health
and by his wounds we are healed.
We had all strayed like sheep,
each of us going his own way,
but the LORD laid on him
the guilt of us all.
He was maltreated, yet he was
    submissive
and did not open his mouth;
like a sheep led to the slaughter,
like a ewe that is dumb before the
    shearers,
he did not open his mouth.
He was arrested and sentenced and
    taken away,
and who gave a thought to his fate—
how he was cut off from the world of
    the living,
stricken to death for my people's
    transgression?
He was assigned a grave with the
    wicked,
a burial-place among felons,

though he had done no violence,
had spoken no word of treachery.
Yet the LORD took thought for his
  oppressed servant
and healed him who had given himself
  as a sacrifice for sin.
He will enjoy long life and see his
  children's children,
and in his hand the LORD's purpose
  will prosper.
By his humiliation my servant will
  justify many;

after his suffering he will see light and
  be satisfied;
it is their guilt he bears.
Therefore I shall allot him a portion
  with the great,
and he will share the spoil with the
  mighty,
because he exposed himself to death
and was reckoned among
  transgressors,
for he bore the sin of many
and interceded for transgressors.

Comments on the Story

This reading is the fourth and last of the Servant Songs. Isaiah 53 could probably win a contest for the title of The Most Debated Chapter of the Bible. The reader is left to ask the question, "Who could this be about?" In fact, this same question is asked in the Bible. In Acts 8:32-34, a person who is not yet a Christian asks the question. Over the ages, untold persons of all backgrounds and interests have asked that same question.

For the commentary here, the identity of the Servant will not be so important as the role and features that relate to that servant. There is more than enough to occupy the storyteller in those aspects. Of course, for the Christian, the very fact that in many congregations the passage is read every Good Friday, and only on Good Friday, is enough to lead to the traditional application for any storyteller.

Paying attention to the change of speakers in this song may be an aid to both understand and retell the story in this passage. In two of the previous songs, the Servant spoke about the call and the task ahead. This song begins and ends with God speaking, while in between these two speeches a chorus, identified simply as "we," speaks many lines, the greatest percentage of lines in the entire song.

God's first speech begins with the declaration that the Servant will surely be successful. He will be "high and exalted," virtually the very words used in Isaiah 6:1 when that prophet sees Yahweh as the king enthroned in the temple. Could the allusion be other than deliberate? This final depiction of the Servant begins with this striking parallel to Isaiah's vision of God.

The REB differs from many other translations in two ways at 52:14. First, it introduces the phrase "my people." It makes this insertion, allowing a particular interpretation of the masculine singular "you." Second, the REB retains the masculine singular "you" the way it is in the standard Hebrew texts, rather than changing it to "him" (as do two ancient Hebrew manuscripts and the ancient Aramaic and Syriac translations). In this way, there is a contrast between Israel ("my people") and the Servant ("him," who might still be "the ideal Israel").

Kings and nations will see the gross disfigurement of the Servant. The description is puzzling. The speaker (God) does not tell precisely why the Servant is so deformed and stigmatized. The speakers do say that this event and experience are brand new; no one has ever seen or dreamed these things before this occasion.

In 53:1 the "we" begin their ten-verse speech. They pick up exactly where the preceding verses left off. This event is incredible to the ordinary person, and it must be seen as an act of God.

It is somewhat surprising that the poet writing here does not use more metaphors in this section of the song than those that appear. (Perhaps Second Isaiah, who possessed truly great poetic power, might not be the author of these lines.) "Young plant" and "sheep" are the similes that appear in an otherwise apparently straightforward and specific account of the sufferings and death of the person identified as "Servant."

Although metaphor and simile do not dominate the presentation, there are images or ideas that do hover over and dwell in the words, and these two ideas are sacrifice and substitution.

The offering for sin was a standard part of the religion of ancient Israel. Sacrifices were of various kinds and were offered for many reasons. Sin offerings were those by which the sinners were restored to friendship with God. The Servant is declared to make this kind of sacrifice. He takes on himself the sins and the burdens, the guilt and the need for restoration with God that belonged to others.

The speakers are in awe of the generosity of this action. The novelty and incredible graciousness of this move have struck the speakers in the song (and had already struck the writer of the song).

The idea that someone else can substitute for an individual or a group in these matters is virtually unheard of in the writings of ancient Israel. The fact that this person will be a substitute for the people, accomplishing what they could not do, truly amazes the group that speaks. They confess their sins by admitting that the Servant suffers in their place.

The chorus's description of the Servant's sufferings is overwhelming. The disfigurement and unappealing features of the man repulse all people. Only those for whom he has suffered are willing to think or speak about him. Interpreters have thought of leprosy or some other kind of skin disease for some of the description. Perhaps more horrible are the torture and physical abuse inflicted on the Servant.

Naming God as the source of this suffering is alarming. The idea that undeserved suffering might come from God is central to the book of Job. There Job insists that God has sent his sufferings without any basis. Here the suffering is given to an innocent person but clearly on behalf of others. Here no charge of arbitrariness exists.

To some commentators, it is not obvious whether the Servant suffers death. For many readers, the mention of a burial place is convincing: Only the dead are buried. The new life beyond the grave would be continuation of the work that the Servant did. He would live on in those who had accepted his ideas and were fired with the fervor that fired him.

This Servant is clearly a unique figure in biblical literature. The storyteller has no difficulty in identifying with the chorus, the "we" in verses 1-10. The debates about the identity of the figure in the text have not yet died. Indeed, the figure may remain enigmatic for some readers.

For this commentator, the Servant is the prophet, the one we call Second Isaiah. The three previous Servant Songs tell, in various voices, of the role and message of salvation that the prophet has for the people. The message of liberation was not accepted by the fellow exiles, and the Servant was maligned, arrested, and executed. The chorus in this last song is the group of people who had given the prophet some acceptance, but who witnessed the rejection of the message by the exiles as a whole and eventually witnessed the sufferings that the prophet underwent because of the message. But the message does live on in those who accept it and in the writings that remain (which have now become Isaiah 40–55).

This proposal is not the only interpretation possible for the historical Servant. Others see the Servant as a metaphor for Israel, the people of God who suffered immensely in the exile. Others propose that the Servant is the ideal Israel who is sent to the people to purge them of their unfaithfulness. Israel is to be the light to the nations. The nations will benefit from the sufferings that persecuted Israel has suffered.

For most Christian readers, the historical Servant is not the major focus of their reading. Indeed, few Christians will hear these words without applying them to the Lord of their own faith. He who suffered death is presented as victorious over death in order that his followers throughout the centuries may share in that victory.

Retelling the Story

Grandpa Cabbagehead, we called him. No one remembered where the name came from or who stuck it on him first. Some of the elders said it came from the time when his mule died, and he walked all the way into town to sell his produce at market, carrying the vegetables in a heavy sack. Others said it was because of his looks; his face was oddly arranged, nose out of joint and a shapeless chin. Still others insisted that the name matched his mind. He seemed as innocent of grown-up thought as a newborn. So the name meant his head was thick as a cabbage or perhaps that his mother had, in fact, found him in a cabbage patch.

He never married, and no one knew exactly how old he had been when he and his mother moved to the little place at the curve of the road. They called their place Burning Springs, but no one paid it much mind.

After his mother had gone on to glory, he seemed a bit lost, but his clothes were always clean and neat on Sunday. Since he was the way he was, he never got to be a deacon, but they did let him help take the collection. And those who shared a pew with him every so often said he had a surprisingly nice voice when he sang.

His farm was perched between two hills, so he and the mule had to work hard to stay upright when they plowed. It was known to be poor land, so how he managed to grow what he grew no one knew. He canned tomatoes, corn, beans, potatoes, berries, and squash. The jars were neatly stacked under the cellar stairs, more than one man could eat. Whenever a baby was born or a mother laid up sick, a sack of glass jars would show up at the door, filled with the stuff of his garden.

It was hard to find work in those parts. Farming kept food on the table, but didn't go far toward providing shoes for the feet under that table. Men would travel as far as Cleveland to look for jobs, but if they found them, trouble seemed close behind. To work in a factory, away from the sun, went against the grain of mountain minds. Sometimes the whole family would up and move away, but the stories of drinking and fighting would drift back down to those left behind.

As times grew leaner, the preacher preached on holding together with hard work and prayer, but the men stood around the church door and worried their hats and shifted their chews. They were doing all they could, but it wasn't enough. Grandpa Cabbagehead stood with them, but never said a word.

Early one morning, he could be seen dressed in his Sunday clothes and heading west. By the third day, the gossip had turned to worry. What if he was lost or hurt or worse? He wasn't much, but he was familiar. The women recounted the countless jars of food that had kept them fed. The men remembered how he always showed up to lend a hand when the crops were ready and help was hard to find. Nobody had a memory of returning the favor to boast of, so they fussed over his absence.

The fourth day after he had left, Grandpa Cabbagehead returned, but he didn't return alone. Riding in a

> The ancient rabbis took this passage to mean that suffering was not a sign of God's displeasure, much less a punishment for individual or corporate sins. Rather, sometimes suffering can be seen as a sign of God's favor. To speak a word for God to people who have no desire to listen can frequently bring about suffering. Ask any prophet. (*Sefer Ha-Aggadah* 717.310)

truck that was pulling a load of strange-looking machines, stuck between two big men, he merely nodded to his neighbors as he passed. The relief from worry turned a trifle sour when he didn't stop to explain himself, but after two days, curiosity drove several neighbors up the hollow between the hills.

The men had set up a drill, and one of them shared the news that oil had been discovered, just where the old man had said it would be found. They were the ones who announced how big this strike might be, and what the going rate was, and yes, the company could always use some hardworking men. Grandpa Cabbagehead just stood and listened.

Now, you might think that that news would have cheered the whole community right down to its socks. However, it went the other way, it seems. Oh, the people were glad for the work when it came, but what was God thinking about to dump that oil under the soil of a man like that? What would he do with all the money? He had only himself to care for—and so the talk went. People would fall silent when the old man came near. The men voted to make him deacon of the church, but they no longer shared their tobacco with him as they stood by the church door, waiting for their women to finish up.

There's no telling what might have happened if the feelings kept on that way. But one morning he wasn't to be found in his field or on his porch or down by the new well that was pumping. His closest neighbor, Deacon Wills, knocked on his door and finally went in. Everything was neat, apple-pie order, but the family Bible, his Sunday suit, and his mother's picture were missing. On the kitchen table was a piece of paper, a deed for the land and the oil contract made out to the whole community. On the paper he'd simply written, "Make yourselves at home."

His place is like a shrine now, kept spotlessly clean, ready in case he ever comes back. And the one thing you can say about us now is that we are friendly folks. We treat neighbor and stranger really well. But even our children will stand at the side of the road several times a day, restless, hoping, and watching. *(Heather Murray Elkins)*

The Drink Vendor

Free products are offered so that the people will pay attention to promises of God's deliverance.

The Story

Come for water, all who are thirsty;
though you have no money, come,
buy grain and eat;
come, buy wine and milk,
not for money, not for a price.
Why spend your money for what is not
food,
your earnings on what fails to satisfy?
Listen to me and you will fare well,
you will enjoy the fat of the land.
Come to me and listen to my words,
hear me and you will have life:
I shall make an everlasting covenant
with you
to love you faithfully as I loved David.
I appointed him a witness to peoples,
a prince ruling over them;
and you in turn will summon nations
you do not know,
and nations that do not know you will
hasten to you,
because the LORD your God,
Israel's Holy One, has made you
glorious.
Seek the LORD while he is present,
call to him while he is close at hand.
Let the wicked abandon their ways
and the evil their thoughts:
let them return to the LORD, who will
take pity on them,
and to our God, for he will freely
forgive.
For my thoughts are not your
thoughts,
nor are your ways my ways.
This is the word of the LORD.
But as the heavens are high above the
earth,
so are my ways high above your ways
and my thoughts above your thoughts.
As the rain and snow come down from
the heavens
and do not return there without
watering the earth,
making it produce grain
to give seed for sowing and bread to
eat,
so is it with my word issuing from my
mouth;
it will not return to me empty
without accomplishing my purpose
and succeeding in the task for which I
sent it.
You will go out with joy
and be led forth in peace.
Before you mountains and hills will
break into cries of joy,
and all the trees in the countryside
will clap their hands.
Pine trees will grow in place of
camel-thorn,
myrtles instead of briars;
all this will be a memorial for the
LORD,
a sign that for all time will not be cut
off.

Comments on the Story

This passage opens with a most attractive invitation. It is no wonder that it has been chosen as the lection for one of the most solemn and inspiring moments of the liturgy. We are lucky to have at the Easter Vigil this reading, which depicts pure graciousness and bounteous generosity.

The shouts with which the passage opens, "Come" and "Come, buy," have been likened to those of a street merchant. In the larger towns of the Middle East even today one can readily meet a drink merchant who carries his product on his back in an elaborately decorated metal container. He bows over to pour out his sale into a vessel for the buyer, who consumes it on the spot.

The merchant who cries out in this reading, however, is not selling; he is giving his product away. He charges nothing of the person who really wants the drink. And who wouldn't need a drink on those hot, dry days in the streets of Jerusalem or Damascus? "Come, buy without money!" Surely an unheard-of offer. The prophet is trying to startle his readers. He startles even us near the turn of the twenty-first century.

There is another proposal of the source from which the prophet got the idea for this figure. The invitation has also been likened to the behest of Lady Wisdom (Prov. 9:5), who does not want the young to go without that which can fulfill them. Unlike most sellers, but like the drink merchant in the first interpretation, she offers her substance free of charge.

The opening, then, is a surprise in many ways. Whether it is Lady Wisdom or a drink vendor (surely this picturesque fellow should be noticed by the storyteller), the speech in Hebrew opens with a curious word, *hoy,* the word that in prophetic judgment oracles is often translated "woe [to]." The use of this word in such an oracle arose from the cry of grief of a mourner in the presence of a corpse. This meaning is out of the question here, however. The RSV and the NRSV translate it here as "Ho," following the KJV.

In verse 3, God speaks directly to the people of the goal to make a covenant with them. The experience of exile led most thinkers to the conclusion that the Sinai covenant was broken (see Psalm 89; Jer. 31:32). The covenant that this prophet now speaks of is a reaffirmation of the covenant God made with David.

Many interpreters speak of, for this passage, the reinterpretation of that covenant. The covenant with Jerusalem's only dynasty is here broadened to include the whole people. The unconditional nature of the Davidic covenant here replaces the covenant with Israel, which, in essence, depended on whether Israel chose God and remained faithful. Now the whole people, together and individually, share in what once was the sphere of the king and the dynasty. The "you" in verse 5 is in the singular, while verses 1-4, 6, and 8-9 are addressed to a group. Verse 5, then, is a highpoint of egalitarianism for the biblical people. An American storyteller might focus here.

Yet there is another surprise. David became a leader of neighboring peoples; accordingly, the prophet proclaims that Israel is to become a leader of peoples, the one who is to bring them to the God of Israel. Even people whom Israel had not yet known eventually will be brought to God through this Israel.

The whole chapter may be viewed as God's speech. The only interruption is the prophet's address to the people in verses 6-7. "Seek the Lord," he cries. For the prophets of the eighth century B.C.E., and perhaps later, this command is a call to offer sacrifice. God is sought by the correct offering in the temple. But the prophet of the exile means something more than a correct altar and the right sacrifice, for no sacrifice was possible in the exile. The prophet seems to call for a more internal turning to God, a gift of the heart, of the self. God, who is all merciful, looks for true seekers, people who hunger for God.

The speech of God returns in verse 8 with the statement that God's thoughts and ways are radically different from those of human beings. Almost as if the book were following Aristotelian logic, the next idea is the effect of God's creative word/thought. God's word is a creative, effective word, and one can compare its effectiveness to the rain in its irresistible fall to the earth and its eventual return to the heavens.

This proclamation of the effectiveness of the word of God parallels the proclamation of the word of God in Isaiah 40:8. This theme of the word of God as framing the words of Second Isaiah suggests that there was deliberate editing of these chapters. As proposed earlier, chapters 41–48 and 49–55 form two separate collections, each dominated by a major image. Israel, the people, is the addressee in 41–48, while 49–55 is addressed to the city under the name Zion or Jerusalem.

The chapter ends with the renewed assurance that the exiles will return home. The inevitability of the result of God's project to return the exiles home is the thrust of the whole chapter. The way home is the one called for in chapter 40. The highway and the messengers of peace nicely parallel in both chapters 40 and 55.

The prophet wants to find the most moving expression for the joy that will accompany the exiles, so he chooses to see the mountains and the trees burst into animation, exaltation, and celebration. (What storyteller could pass up these lovely trees clapping their "hands"?) Different parts of nature burst into praise in Psalms 96:11-12 and 98:7-8 for the Creator King who also judges. This prophet depicts all of nature rejoicing in the freedom that the people will experience.

Retelling the Story

At the heart of the bazaar, the rug merchant spread his wares, richly woven carpets of every hue. The market's kaleidoscope of sights and sounds was the perfect setting for the woven visions that he unfolded in the open air. Even the most cynical of shoppers were caught by the jewel-like tones of the rugs. The back and forth of bargaining added to the noisy clamor. Men and women, rich and poor, made their way to the rug merchant's stall. Some left with a treasure rolled under their arm, beaming with the bargains they discovered. And some departed angry and empty-handed, complaining loudly about the impossible cost. But the rug merchant seemed content with either choice.

When the late afternoon sun reached into the stalls, some of the merchants began to collect their wares. The rug merchant waited, patiently, for the last of the sun and the final customer of the day. A well-dressed woman stopped by, fingering the wool. The rug dealer waited and watched as the woman flipped through the rugs that were unrolled. "What is the price of this one?" she asked.

"Ten thousand dollars," he answered her.

She dropped that rug and moved to another. "And this?"

"Oh, that one. Five hundred dollars."

She frowned and inspected the two rugs. They looked nearly identical. "And how much is this one?"

"Twenty-five dollars."

"Twenty-five dollars!" Now she circled the rolled up rugs, confused and eager at the same time. "Why is there such a difference in price? I mean, this one looks like that one. Is there a difference in the wool, in the weaver? Why is one so expensive and one so cheap?" The rug dealer merely shrugged and replied, "What is a price but a question of beauty?"

> When Isaiah invites us to come to the "water," the sages say he is drawing a comparison between the Torah and water. Like water, the Torah refreshes. Like water, there would be no life without Torah. As water cleans our bodies, so Torah cleans our spirits. As rainfall is sometimes accompanied by rumblings of thunder, so too is the study of Torah. They add this warning, however. Just as someone unaccustomed to water can drown, so can Torah consume those inexperienced in its study. (*Song of Songs Rabbah* 1.2 [3] and *Sefer Ha-Aggadah* 404.22)

The woman shook her head, her eyes continuing to circle the woven art that represented hundreds of hours of human labor and centuries of human culture. "How much for these two rugs?"

The rug merchant smiled. "Five hundred dollars for both."

Now she began to circle the rugs, her fingers greedy, her eyes narrowed like those of a cat stalking a bird. "How much for these three, no, these four?"

"Ah, lady," said the rug merchant, "I will let you have all the rugs for the price of this one, five hundred dollars." The shock of his answer stopped her circling. She wavered back and forth between doubt and greed, hope and fear. She pulled out her purse, then stuffed it back in her pocket again. Three times she repeated this in and out, yes and no while the merchant sat and watched her, patient as the sun went down.

"Tomorrow. Tomorrow, I will be back for my rugs." With that, she straightened and surveyed her kingdom of carpet. "Tomorrow, I will return and buy all of these for five hundred dollars." And she smiled to herself as she made her way through the narrow aisles of stalls. The rug merchant smiled as well as he rolled up his rugs for the night. Bright and early, the woman returned to acquire her treasure, secured for a ridiculous price. But there was no sign of the merchant, and no one seemed to know where he'd gone or when he'd come again. *(Heather Murray Elkins)*

> If someone were to fall off the roof of a house, it is likely that the attending physicians would have to treat all the injured parts of the body differently. God does not work that way, according to the rabbis. Though the ear is only one of many parts of the body, if we will listen to God, we will live. (*Exodus Rabbah* 27.9)

The Eunuch and the Gentile

After the exile, God will accept all people—even those who are less than perfect.

The Story

THESE are the words of the LORD:
Maintain justice, and do what is
right;
for my deliverance is close at hand,
and my victory will soon be revealed.
Happy is the person who follows
these precepts
and holds fast to them,
who keeps the sabbath unprofaned,
who keeps his hand from all
wrongdoing!
The foreigner who has given his
allegiance to the LORD must not
say,
'The LORD will exclude me from his
people.'
The eunuch must not say,
'I am naught but a barren tree.'
These are the words of the LORD:
The eunuchs who keep my sabbaths,
who choose to do my will
and hold fast to my covenant,
will receive from me something better
than sons and daughters,
a memorial and a name in my own
house and within my walls;
I shall give them everlasting renown,
an imperishable name.
So too with the foreigners who give
their allegiance to me,
to minister to me and love my name
and become my servants,
all who keep the sabbath unprofaned
and hold fast to my covenant:
these I shall bring to my holy hill
and give them joy in my house of
prayer.
Their offerings and sacrifices
will be acceptable on my altar;
for my house will be called
a house of prayer for all nations.
This is the word of the Lord GOD,
who gathers those driven out of Israel:
I shall add to those who have already
been gathered.

Comments on the Story

Isaiah 56–66 is generally referred to as Third Isaiah. The use of this term, however, differs from the way "Second Isaiah" is used. Isaiah 40–55 is far more unified than is Isaiah 56–66, and Isaiah 40–55 reads as though it were written by one person. Many commentators consider Third Isaiah to be a collection of oracles uttered by various prophets over a period of time in the postexilic era. The exiles had already returned home; the general thrust of the message of Second Isaiah had come true.

89

The entirety of Second Isaiah's vision has not materialized. There was no return to Eden. Real problems of the postexilic time included many different areas. Recent commentators have used passages in Third Isaiah to illustrate specific tensions within the postexilic setting. The returning exiles, most of whom probably had never lived in Jerusalem, having been born in Babylon, now claim precedence of status and power over those Jews who had not been deported. The deportees had included the priestly families who now preside in the rebuilt Temple.

This opening section from Third Isaiah is illustrative of certain problems of the time. The passage addresses groups of people who have traditionally been excluded from the Temple; specifically, eunuchs and foreigners were excluded from entry into the holy place. Each group had its own reason for exclusion. Eunuchs were understood to be deformed or maimed. The thought of the time was that since God deserved only the best, God could be approached only by a full human being, not some inadequate remains from some accident. This restriction on human beings parallels a rule of sacrifice. An animal that was misshapen or marred could not be offered to God. So, too, eunuchs, who were seen as incomplete, were to be kept from the presence of God.

Foreigners were persons who did not trace physical descent from the common ancestors the people claimed. These outsiders, too, were not to be admitted to the presence of the God of Israel. The Temple layout made this quite clear. It had three courts: the court of the peoples, the court of Israel, and the court of the men. Only within this last court was the Holy of Holies, the dwelling of God. A foreigner was thus thrice-removed from the Holy of Holies, where the divine resided.

This prophetic passage challenges that idea. It contradicts the older position that holds that physical characteristics or foreign birth would disqualify one from the presence of Yahweh. The prophet proclaims that access to God is open to all who accept God and God's demands for justice.

The radicalness of the passage is helped by reflecting on verses 2-5. Verse 3 puts both groups together in their complaint of being left out. The foreign born who has chosen the God of Israel must not feel excluded, and the eunuch who acknowledges Yahweh must not feel unfulfilled.

Another reason for looking at these verses is that they are the source of the name of a renowned institution. The text says that the faithful eunuchs will receive from the Lord "something better than sons and daughters." They will receive "a memorial and a name in my own house and within my walls" (v. 5). The "memorial and name" in Hebrew are *Yad Vashem*. These Hebrew words have become the name of the museum and other components of the Holocaust Martyrs' and Heroes' Remembrance Authority in Jerusalem. Jews worldwide recall those Jews in Eastern Europe who were exterminated by the Nazi regime during the years when they controlled Germany.

The section on the foreigners, or "those driven out of Israel" (vv. 6-8), focuses on the Temple. Obviously, then, the passage was written after 515 B.C.E., the date of the dedication of the restored Temple.

The test of the fidelity of these people includes giving "allegiance to me," "minister to me and love my name," "keep the sabbath unprofaned," and "hold fast to my covenant." (The REB has "the Lord" in parts of this verse instead of the first person singular in the Hebrew—on the supposition that a scribe mistook a Hebrew letter for an abbreviation of the divine name.) Two aspects can be commented on.

The observance of the sabbath is a practice that was in use perhaps during the time of the monarchy. But it is with the exile, when the people are deprived of the Temple, of sacrifice, and of kingship, that the community began to focus on this particular element, which was not connected with Temple or king, to maintain this people's distinctive religious identity.

The idea of covenant, too, may have undergone an exilic expansion. The eighth-century B.C.E. prophets do not mention the Sinai covenant. The people's relationship with God is expressed in other metaphors. Later, the book of Jeremiah has the most covenant-oriented passages in the Prophets, especially in those parts that are heavily influenced by the ideas of the book of Deuteronomy. In the exile, Second Isaiah referred to the Davidic covenant. Here in the postexilic period, Third Isaiah seems to sum up the whole varied tradition in simply "my covenant."

Surely the astounding thing in the passage is the inclusion in the covenant-community of those who had been excluded by tradition or by the tensions of the new postexilic environment. Those who in no way could earlier claim the priesthood and privileges now are being promised full participation in groups that were once elitist.

Retelling the Story

The church sign said:

SERVICE AT 11:00
EVERYONE WELCOME
"But I couldn't get into the sanctuary without the ushers lifting my wheelchair. There wasn't room in the aisle except on the first row. No one else sat in front of the tenth row. No one spoke to me, either. I don't think I'll go back there. I must have failed to read the small print on the sign: 'Except for people in wheelchairs.' "

ALL ARE WELCOME
"I stood across the street and watched the people go into the church

building. Everyone was dressed to kill. Not one person wore jeans. Rich, too, they looked. I shoved my hands into my pockets to warm them up. Maybe next week I'll have enough guts to go inside for the service. Don't know what they would say. I hate to be stared at. I haven't gotten over that time I went to a church and they wouldn't let me in. I guess I'll have my Sunday service in the park again."

WE WELCOME YOU

"Me? You welcome me? I've tried to worship at churches like this. It's usually okay for a while. 'Nice, good-looking young man. Isn't it nice to have Tom here? I have a niece I'd love for you to meet. Do you have any family here?' I just get sick of having to lie about myself at church. I wish I could tell them about my family here. But he doesn't go to church. He says, 'Why do you waste your time with those hypocrites? They wouldn't care anything about you if they knew who you really were.' He's right. I usually end up dropping out of church and wondering whether there will ever be a place for me."

COME AND WORSHIP

"We just moved into this neighborhood from another city. My husband was on the board of our other church. I'd like to join a church here in the neighborhood. It would be good for the children to be able to go to the choirs and the summer activities. But I don't know. We asked for a call from the pastor. He came, but he seemed cool. He said that the church had a family like us once before, and they sure could sing spirituals. When my husband stopped by to see the facilities, the secretary thought he was there to ask for money.

"I don't want to have to fight another battle just to go to church. We'll probably join the church that one of my co-workers attends. It's across town, but we'll truly be welcome there."

A HOUSE OF PRAYER FOR ALL PEOPLES

"Everyone is welcome here. God has issued the invitation. All who join themselves to God are acceptable. The foreigner and the eunuch. Those named outcast and unacceptable. Saints and sinners. The poor and the rich, the young and the old. Baptist and Methodist, Pentecostal, Unitarian, and Catholic. Married and single, heterosexual and gay. Black and white and brown, indigenous and immigrant.

"All who love the name of the Lord, who join themselves to God, are accepted and forgiven at the altar. Welcome to the sanctuary for all peoples. All are invited to the welcome table, God's feast of hospitality, the messianic banquet."

92

Thus says the Lord God, who gathers the outcasts and welcomes them to the house of prayer. *(Beth Richardson)*

The sages say that Isaiah incorporated all 613 commandments in one sentence of two parts. The prophet said, "Maintain justice, and do what is right" (56:1). That just about sums it up. (*Sefer Ha-Aggadah* 463.567)

The Proper Fast

Fasting is not pursued for interior gratification but for the sake of others.

The Story

S hout aloud without restraint;
lift up your voice like a trumpet.
Declare to my people their
 transgression,
to the house of Jacob their sins,
although they ask guidance of me day
 after day
and say they delight in knowing my
 ways.
As if they were a nation which had
 acted rightly
and had not abandoned the just laws
 of their God,
they ask me for righteous laws
and delight in approaching God.
'Why should we fast, if you ignore it?
Why mortify ourselves, if you pay no
 heed?'
In fact you serve your own interests on
 your fast-day
and keep all your men hard at work.
Your fasting leads only to wrangling
 and strife
and to lashing out with vicious blows.
On such a day the fast you are keeping
is not one that will carry your voice to
 heaven.
Is this the kind of fast that I require,
a day of mortification such as this:
that a person should bow his head like
 a bulrush
and use sackcloth and ashes for a
 bed?
Is that what you call a fast,
a day acceptable to the LORD?
Rather, is not this the fast I require:
to loose the fetters of injustice,
to untie the knots of the yoke,
and set free those who are oppressed,
tearing off every yoke?
Is it not sharing your food with the
 hungry,
taking the homeless poor into your
 house,
clothing the naked when you meet
 them,
and never evading a duty to your
 kinsfolk?
Then your light will break forth like
 the dawn,
and new skin will speedily grow over
 your wound;
your righteousness will be your
 vanguard
and the glory of the LORD your
 rearguard.
Then, when you call, the LORD will
 answer;
when you cry to him, he will say, 'Here
 I am.'
If you cease to pervert justice,
to point the accusing finger and lay
 false charges,
If you give of your own food to the
 hungry
and satisfy the needs of the wretched,
then light will rise for you out of
 darkness

and dusk will be for you like noonday;
the LORD will be your guide
  continually
and will satisfy your needs in the bare
  desert;
he will give you strength of limb;
you will be like a well-watered garden,
like a spring whose waters never fail.
Buildings long in ruins will be restored
  by your own kindred
and you will build on ancient
  foundations;
you will be called the rebuilder of
  broken walls,
the restorer of houses in ruins.
If you refrain from sabbath journeys
and from doing business on my holy
  day,
if you call the sabbath a day of joy
and the LORD's holy day worthy of
  honour,
if you honour it by desisting from work
and not pursuing your own interests
  or attending to your own affairs,
then you will find your joy in the
  LORD,
and I shall make you ride on the
  heights of the earth,
and the holding of your father Jacob
  will be yours to enjoy.
The LORD himself has spoken.

Comments on the Story

This passage can be read as a kind of treatise on true religion or as a polemic within the tensions of the postexilic community. Probably the two approaches are not completely mutually exclusive. The difference between these approaches need not worry the reader or the reteller. Regardless of how the biblical text arose, the spirit of God can still speak through it.

As a treatise on true religion, the overwhelming emphasis falls on the interior of the person. (The imitation of a prophet's call in v. 1 gives added solemnity and significance to the passage.) All external rites and rituals are of little avail if the person's interior is not directed to God. One can have the outward appearance of proper religious behavior and knowledge and still not truly be turned to God. Even the seeking of "righteous laws," admirable in itself, is no guarantor of true devotion of the heart.

Even so convincing a practice as that of fasting is not an automatic mark that those who do this please God. Fasting in Israel, in fact, became a more widely practiced religious custom in the postexilic time. The preexilic fasting that we find often served as a sign of mourning and occasionally was a means of petitioning a favor. In this postexilic passage, fasting is understood as a way of getting God's attention and goodwill.

Fasting is first mentioned here in the context of an accusation against "my people." The identity of the speaker is not obvious. The speaker may well be one of those who has been ostracized from the postexilic power structure. Then "my people" would have an ironic ring to it. The people of God have abandoned the principles of that God. And this prophetic voice speaks to ensure that the oppressed will not be forgotten.

The description of fasting and its effects is almost humorous. Fasting is meant to turn God's attention toward those who engage in this penitential practice. Instead, the fasting leads to dissent and bitter conflicts among the people. It is no wonder that God does not want to look at them.

In verse 5 the "you" shifts from plural to singular and remains thus throughout the chapter. Moreover, the author begins to redefine the word *fast*. The prophet declares with the voice of God those things that really catch the eye of God: "to loose the fetters of injustice,/ to untie the knots of the yoke,/ and set free those who are oppressed."

The things that really delight God in verse 7 are all directed to one's fellow human beings. They deal with offering physical care to the person in need. When one does these works of mercy, the promise is that God will respond with the cry that God expects of true worshipers, "Here I am."

When the person truly cares for the neighbor, already a time like the time of fulfillment comes. Light, healing, even the glory of the Lord will come to that person.

Full restoration in the early postexilic times would be the rebuilding of the city of Jerusalem. This restoration will take place to such a degree and with such enthusiasm that the individual, astoundingly, will get new titles: "Rebuilder of Broken Walls" and "Restorer of Houses in Ruins"—certainly titles that people in postexilic Jerusalem would treasure.

In the closing verses, the religious practice that appears is not fasting but the full participation in the sabbath observances and rest. The holiness of the seventh day, the last day of the week, had already become quite common for the postexilic Jews. Although the sabbath had been observed in the preexilic community, the exile made it a defining element of the religious identity of the Jew.

Sabbath is the day of rest devoted to the study of God's ways (and, later, to the study of God's word). Business and busyness are to be set aside in order for one to become more available to the Lord. In this text, sabbath observance seems to be a private or individual thing. Subsequent Judaism stressed the communal and especially familial observance of the sabbath.

The promise attached to observance might also sound individual, "the holding [heritage] of your father Jacob will be yours to enjoy." But this statement and the whole verse seem to be a reference to Deuteronomy 32:13. The author consciously alludes to the promises that the readers already know from the written tradition. Prophecy is becoming (or has already become) a written medium more than a spoken one.

The reteller might focus on the "newness" in the passage: the new prophet, the new meaning of *fast*, the new building on the old foundations, and the new names presented to the surprised readers.

Retelling the Story

"What is 'good enough' for God?" the young preacher stood before the small congregation and asked. "We come to worship. We pray. We give our tithe. We go to Sunday school. In the fall we bring canned food for the food bank. Is that good enough for God?"

Some in the congregation coughed and shifted in their pews. "Here we go again—more new ideas from this new preacher." "I liked it better when we had one of those old guys close to retirement. Friendly, easy-going, not too many new ideas." "What is she saying? That we're not doing enough? I've done more than anybody else for years—since before she was born. The nerve!"

The preacher read from Isaiah 58 and continued. "The prophet Isaiah talks about religious people who do all the right things—they fast, and they observe the sabbath. They pray and practice righteousness. They draw near to God, and they wonder why God does not notice them. We're doing it right, God. Isn't this enough?

"What Isaiah said to the church members of that day was, 'No, it's not enough for you just to fast and practice your righteousness.' Isaiah says that God is asking for a new kind of fast, one that goes beyond sackcloth and ashes. Isaiah proclaims a new kind of fast: 'To loose the bonds of injustice,/ to undo the thongs of the yoke,/ to let the oppressed go free . . . to share your bread with the hungry,/ and bring the homeless poor into your house' [Isa. 58:6-7, NRSV]."

"Uh-oh, now you're meddling," the collective thought shot back toward the pulpit. "We do enough. We let that group of alcoholics meet here on Friday nights. And Sarah has gone over to the Catholic church to help serve meals to those homeless people. And we gave over $500 to missions last year."

> When is the appropriate time to assist the poor and homeless? The sages say whenever they need it. Now is the best time to welcome them. (*Sefer Ha-Aggadah* 666.262)

"What would it be like," the preacher asked, "if this church took up the kind of fast that Isaiah is talking about? What would our congregation look like? Would we have homeless people sleeping here during the winter? Would we have neighborhood children coming here after school? Would we open our doors to the people who have never set foot in our building before? The poor, the homeless, persons of color, unmarried mothers, people who struggle with addictions—these are the people that Isaiah is talking about."

"Last time we let the neighborhood kids in, they wrecked the nursery." "We don't have enough in the budget to take care of all these people. We have to take care of the church building, after all." "We've never had black people here in our church. They'd probably be happier with their own kind." "What is she trying to do? Ruin our church!"

"What is good enough?" the preacher asked. "What is a fast that is acceptable to God? These questions are hard, I know. It's not easy to change when we don't have to. It's not easy to do things a new way. But God did not promise that the way would be easy. God promised that we would never be alone along the way. Being faithful to God is hard, hard work.

"Isaiah proclaimed that if we satisfy the needs of the afflicted, then God will guide us and satisfy our needs and make us strong. 'You shall be like a watered garden,/ like a spring of water,/ whose waters never fail' [Isa. 58:11, NRSV]. I invite the church to think about what Isaiah said. What is good enough for God? What are the signs of our faithfulness to God? What is the fast that this congregation is being called to?"

"I don't know. . . . I'm too old for this. Maybe the young ones in the congregation can do something." "I hate it when she preaches out of the Bible. Something like this always gets stirred up." "I wonder what is good enough for God. Am I doing enough? And if I'm not doing enough, will I have enough courage and energy to do any more? God help us all." *(Beth Richardson)*

Why does Isaiah say that God's light will break forth like the dawn? Well, there is no deeper darkness than just before dawn. If the entire sun were to appear all at once people would be overwhelmed. Rather, a few streaks of light creep across the sky at dawn, the sun peeps over the horizon, and it slowly covers the people with light. Just so the light of God would overwhelm us if it came all at once. That is the reason it will break forth *like the dawn.* (*Sefer Ha-Aggadah* 393.40)

A Mother Welcomes Back Her Children

Jerusalem is thrilled because she can bestow riches on her returning offspring.

The Story

A rise, shine, Jerusalem, for your light has come;
and over you the glory of the Lord has dawned.
Though darkness covers the earth
an dark night the nations,
on you the LORD shines
and over you his glory will appear;
nations will journey towards your light
and kings to your radiance.
Raise your eyes and look around:
they are all assembling, flocking back to you;
your sons are coming from afar,
your daughters walking beside them.
You will see it, and be radiant with joy,
and your heart will thrill with gladness;
sea-borne riches will be lavished on you
and the wealth of nations will be yours.
Camels in droves will cover the land,
young camels from Midian and Ephah,
all coming from Sheba
laden with gold and frankincense,
heralds of the LORD's praise.

Comments on the Story

In this chapter, Third Isaiah takes on a different tone. "Third Isaiah," the writers collected in Isaiah 56–66, living in postexilic times, addresses the concerns of the community that had returned to their city. The trip from Babylon to Jerusalem was exhausting, and, not surprisingly, restoration of the society in the land of Judah was very difficult.

The different oracles in Third Isaiah do not have the unity and cohesiveness that those in Second Isaiah have. An example of this looser coherence is this passage's lack of the practical bent that chapters 56–59 have. Some commentators have suggested that this chapter is actually part of Second Isaiah that was displaced in the transmission of the prophetic words. Alternatively, one can think of chapter 60 (even chapters 61–62) as a reaffirmation of future glory despite the failure of the full restoration predicted by Second Isaiah.

The prophet addresses the city of Jerusalem: "Arise, shine, Jerusalem, for your light has come." The REB and the older liturgical reading in the Roman Catholic tradition have inserted the name "Jerusalem" into the text here to make sure that the addressee is clear. The contrast between light and darkness had appeared already in Isaiah 9:2. Now this contrast is applied to the "she" who is a city. She who was lost and wandering in the dark, she who had nothing of her own but had to seek from any passerby some shred of consolation, she who could claim nothing on her own—she now is told that this situation is changed.

The reteller might think of Cinderella, the one who goes from rags to riches, as a metaphor for Jerusalem because of the pitifulness of its condition. Of course, in Cinderella's story, we can imagine her worthiness from the patience she had in her sufferings. Here, nothing is said of Jerusalem's patience or worthiness.

The promise goes further than mere improvement. Not only will she have a change for the better in her personal life, but also all the nations will see the brilliance of her enlightenment. The sharp contrast between the darkness and the light highlights the reversal of fate in the life of the city.

Zion is depicted as a mother here, as elsewhere in Isaiah 40–66 and also in Psalm 87. She sees her children who have been exiled coming home to her. Both sons and daughters come. The NRSV has a touchingly curious detail, "carried on their nurses' arms." But surely the "return" of the recently born can hardly be considered a return. The REB, on the basis of a cognate Semitic word, has the more understandable "walking beside them." The particular delight Zion takes in the return of her children is charmingly portrayed. One can almost see the smile on her face.

The reference to sea commerce is somewhat surprising. Only Solomon is said to have had merchant fleets. Most likely without even having seen a ship, the author here in Third Isaiah is imagining the contribution of Phoenician marine traders who did indeed travel the whole Mediterranean Sea. Some commentators think that verse 6 is not part of the original writing. If this view is correct, then we can note the skill of the gloss's writer, for the reference to the wondrous caravans from the east and south match the fantastic reference to the sea of the west.

The movement of all the nations to Zion is also striking. Not surprisingly, the universality expressed here has been claimed by Christianity. But the other two Abrahamic faiths claim this idea as well. The idea that Judaism has the vocation to be a moral sounding board for the human race is shared by many Jews. Islam as well has inherited this universality and the emphasis on the applicability of its own message to the whole human race.

Retelling the Story

Early morning dawns. Already, a line of people stretches out as far as the eye can see along the road to Jerusalem. The people are moving slowly under the weight of bags and bundles. Some drive pack animals. Others carry every-thing on their own backs. They carry their possessions, their animals, their babies.

Miriam travels with her husband and baby boy. They have few possessions, and those are carried on the back of a donkey. Miriam's parents died in Baby-lon. But they never gave up hope for returning home. Now, she is fulfilling that dream.

They are exiles returning home. They have survived a dark time and have lived to journey to the light. They have left kinsfolk buried in a foreign land. They also have left many buried hopes and dreams. But now their hope is rekindled, for they are coming home.

They carry heavy packs, but their steps are light, their eyes bright with antic-ipation. Miriam stops and looks around her. She has not seen this land before, but she knows it as if she had been born here. She looks with a thousand eyes at the birthplace of her ancestors. The hearts of the sojourners are full of joy. With each step, they proclaim praise to God.

* * *

"Rise, shine, for thy light is a comin',
My Lord says he's comin' bye and bye."

The southern woods are dark. A small fire burns, lighting the faces of the slaves gathered there for worship. There is singing and praying. The preacher speaks softly and with inten-sity: "The Lord says don't you worry. The Lord's comin' bye and bye. The Lord led the Israelites out of slavery and hardened the pharaoh's heart. The Lord said, 'Let my people go.' Don't you worry, there's going to be freedom for us, too."

The people sing, "Rise, shine, for thy light is a comin'. . . . " At the edge of the circle, Mary feels some-one touch her shoulder. She turns and sees a woman holding a tiny lantern. "Follow me," she says. "It's time."

They creep through the woods. The

> When the Messiah comes, he will make a proclamation from the Temple saying that God has redeemed the people. The sign of that redemption will be the light that shines upon Israel. The light will be upon them alone, but it will serve as a bea-con to the nations. The kings of the nations will come and beg to serve the Messiah because of the light that led them to his presence. (*Sefer Ha-Aggadah* 396.56)

lantern is turned down so the light will not show. They walk, their path illumi-nated by the light of the moon filtering through the trees. As they go, they pick

103

up others along the way. Mary does not know who they are, only that they are fellow travelers on the way to the promised land, on the way to freedom. As she walks, she remembers the preacher's words, "Don't you worry. The Lord's comin' bye and bye." And she feels a little bit of comfort in the midst of her fear.

The pilgrims walk all night across the countryside. The terrain is rough, and the journey is hard. As the sky just begins to lighten, they reach a small farmhouse. Their leader leaves them hidden in the woods and goes up to the barn. There is a light shining inside the barn, and they can see their leader talking to an older man. Soon the signal is given that all is safe and they creep into the barn. Their guide says that she will leave them now. This man will be their conductor for the next part of their journey. But before she leaves, she kneels to pray with them. "Almighty God," she prays, "we are your humble children. Rise and shine your light for these little ones, and keep them safe 'til they reach the promised land. Amen."

As the sun rises, Mary and the others settle into the straw to rest until nighttime.

* * *

"Your sons are coming from afar,
your daughters walking beside them."

In other passages of scripture Israel is compared to an olive tree and God to a lamp. This is because olive oil is employed to burn in a lamp to make light. Just so God and Israel work together to become a light to the nations so they might walk in the right path by the light of their combined efforts. (*Sefer Ha-Aggadah* 393.41)

The mood on the boat is joyful. You can almost touch the excitement. The rails are crowded with refugees watching for land peeking up over the ocean. "We're going home!" The crowd cheers, and a song of praise rises up from the boat. "Praise God, for we are saved. God has driven out the army, and we can come home."

Marie and her father are among the crowd. She was fourteen when they left the shores of Haiti, clinging to a ten-foot raft. They were picked up by the U.S. Coast Guard and taken to a refugee camp at a naval base. Her father did not want to leave Haiti, but he received a message that his life was in danger. He was a leader in their village, trying to help people find food and shelter. They fled in the night to the coast and spent all of their money for passage on the raft. Marie knew that many who left on rafts did not survive the journey.

But now Haiti's president has been restored, and Marie and her father are returning home. Marie's thoughts are on how much more elegant a boat they are returning on than the one in which they left. As she stands on the deck watching the land come closer, she prays to God for peace and harmony for her country. She asks God to bless the leaders and the peasants, to give food to the hungry, and to comfort the ones who have lost so much. May God's light shine on Haiti and all its peoples. *(Beth Richardson)*

Call of the Prophet

Free products are offered so that the people will pay attention to promises of God's deliverance.

The Story

The spirit of the Lord GOD is upon me
because the LORD has anointed me;
he has sent me to announce good
   news to the humble,
to bind up the broken-hearted,
to proclaim liberty to captives,
release to those in prison;
to proclaim a year of the LORD's favour
and a day of the vengeance of our
   God;
to comfort all who mourn,
to give them garlands instead of
   ashes,
oil of gladness instead of mourners'
   tears,
a garment of splendour for the heavy
   heart.
They will be called trees of
   righteousness,
planted by the LORD for his
   adornment.
Buildings long in ruins will be rebuilt
and sites long desolate restored;
they will repair the ruined cities
which for generations have lain
   desolate.

Comments on the Story

In this passage, a figure dramatically gives a self-introduction. This individual has an important role to play in comforting the postexilic community. In a way that seems characteristic of prophecy of this time, the prophet gives a self-definition only in terms of the role to be played rather than by giving a personal name or a communal association. Since a specific identity is unclear, this figure can be easily applied in a variety of situations. In the New Testament, this personage is associated with Jesus (see Luke 4).

In the postexilic community, however, the issue is not whether this is a figure who is still to come, but of how the community is to survive and thrive. This postexilic community needed a prophet like the prophet of the exilic community, the one we call Second Isaiah. But the postexilic community did receive a prophet, or perhaps a group of prophetic writers, whom we collectively call Third Isaiah. These prophets were called to utter words of consolation and encouragement in this new time of trial.

The prophet in this passage is described in images and phrases borrowed from earlier writings. The passage begins with the statement that the Spirit of the Lord has come upon the speaker. This is remarkable in that preexilic prophets rarely invoked the Spirit of God for an understanding of themselves and of their mission. Rather, "the word of the Lord" came to them. The phrase the spirit of the Lord" harks back to the preclassical prophets and to the prophets of salvation who preached security while the classical prophets predicted punishment. This prophet will preach salvation, as the false prophets had preached, but this time the message is from God.

Earlier writings that the depiction of this prophet echoes are the Servant Songs in Isaiah 40–55. This figure is depicted as continuing the work of that servant. He, too, announces good news, binds up the broken-hearted, comforts the mourners, and proclaims release to the captives.

But the different setting means that the same ideas refer to different realities and different people. The last phrase, "to proclaim liberty to captives," suggests a deep problem within the postexilic community. There is a struggle between the persons returning and those who had stayed behind. The returning exiles are depicted as controlling those who had not been deported.

The "humble" and the "broken-hearted," the "captives" and "all who mourn" are not the postexilic community as a whole. They are, rather, those who have lost out in the political and religious struggles of the time of restoration. They receive these prophetic words of encouragement. These are the people who have been excluded and removed from leadership in Jerusalem.

The prophet proclaims a turning of the tables. Things are not going to be as bad as they once were. The expression "a year of the Lord's favour" has been interpreted by many as the Jubilee Year (described in Leviticus 25), at which time the celebration of freedom and redemption would find its fulfillment in the full forgiveness of all debts and release of all people held captive.

Historians cannot tell us whether the Jubilee Year as described in Leviticus was ever really enacted. But it seems clear that this prophet has that kind of glorious and exultant time in mind. The list of replacements for the difficulties of the past rings with joy and newness. Yet each of the new things (garlands, oil of gladness, garment of splendor) are all words and ideas that come from Isaiah 40–55. This writer is well aware of the earlier promises.

Only the "trees of righteousness" are not borrowed from previous writings. The reference might be to the nature worship that the prophets decried. Here the prophet might be overturning that idea, connecting those trees now to the God of Israel and to that God's followers. Or the reference might simply be to the strength and durability of trees. Trees, at least in antiquity, represented something that would withstand trials and last a long time.

The passage closes with the assurance that what had lain waste and in ruin during the exile would now be restored. Cities would be rebuilt, and the community would come to full life. This glorious vision will come true for those who follow the true God. The next verse beyond this reading tells of the foreigners' coming to labor for the people of God. (The writer has an egalitarian spirit but does not extend it to the non-Jew.)

Many commentators point out that this vision of fulfillment did not materialize as hoped within the postexilic community. The visionary and unrealistic aspect of the scene stands out. Since these words of hope and promise did not find literal fulfillment in antiquity, they can serve as a hope for the cities and peoples of today.

The reteller of this passage might focus on the writer and on the presentation of the writer's prophetic figure, or on the figure itself and the good news in the new setting; or the retelling might parallel the narration in Luke 4. For many, this passage still awaits fulfillment.

Retelling the Story

"Go down, Moses, way down in Egypt's land,
Tell old Pharaoh to let my people go."

His family named him Moses. He didn't want to be a preacher, much less a prophet. He wanted to play music. He started playing professionally at the age of twelve, when the bass player for Jackie Wilson came up sick on tour. Moses sat in as a replacement and earned $75, more than his daddy earned in a week's wages. Some of the family thought that this music was the devil's work. But his grandmother taught him about love and justice and his value as a human being.

When the civil rights movement swept his town, he was the one from his family to sit at the lunch counters. His grandmother talked with him about the gospel's promise of freedom for the oppressed. But then, he said, he lost hope. Kennedy and King were assassinated. He became disillusioned and left the church.

Music was his life. His success brought him into the fast lane of the music business—music hits and cocaine, jetting from London to the coast. It didn't stop until he almost died. He promised that he would give his life to God if he survived. And he did.

"Hush, hush, somebody's callin' my name.
Sounds like Jesus, somebody's callin' my name."

He found himself in seminary. He was the first one in his family who ever had to go to seminary to become a preacher. And like that other Moses, God led him where he didn't necessarily want to go. He ended up on the edge of a hill in a small, inner-city church, bringing the good news.

The church had white folk and black folk. It had rich folk and poor. It had alternative folk and straight folk. And it wasn't even governed by his own denomination.

He preached the gospel of freedom and justice and God's love for all people. He sang in the prisons and served lunch to the forgotten. He spoke out about racial bigotry. He challenged those who tried to dominate the other sex. And he grieved over those who would hate and stand in the way of God's love for any reason.

Some folks who knew him before wondered what had happened to him. He might have said, "The spirit of the Lord GOD is upon me . . . to announce good news to the [oppressed]."

He went into the prison and proclaimed a message of freedom and love. A group of prisoners came together to form a gospel group. Moses helped them get a recording contract. He spoke about working with the men in the prison, saying that he knew that it could have been him there as easily as any of them.

> "I've been 'buked and I've been scorned.
> I've been talked about sho's you' born."

Moses was a redeemed prophet, one of those oaks of righteousness. He spoke the truth as he knew it, even if it was troubling to the authorities. He shared his own journey of overcoming addiction and prejudice. And he led people out of the slavery of their own blindness and bigotry.

He lived an "attitude of gratitude," an exuberance in God's generous grace and love. Each Sunday as he stood in the pulpit he said, "It is good to be in the house of the Lord one more time." And all who were present felt that gratitude to the depths of their souls.

> "I will trust in the Lord 'til I die."

One rabbi said that humility was the foremost of virtues and proved his point by quoting Isaiah, "The spirit of the Lord God is upon me because the Lord has anointed me; he has sent me to announce good news to the humble . . ." It was not to the wealthy or important that good news was sent, but to the humble. Thus humility is the first among all fine qualities. (*Sefer Ha-Aggadah* 708.211)

Moses died before seeing the promised land, the fruition of his works. If he had a shortcoming, it was that he took care of others more than he took care of himself. He remains a prophet who calls to the people through the songs he shared—songs of promise, songs of hope, songs of freedom.

"Woke up this morning with my mind, stayed on Jesus. Hallelu, Hallelu, Hallelujah."

(Beth Richardson)

A Chosen People

The prophet invokes all tradition to argue that Israel is preferred by God.

The Story

For I the LORD love justice
and hate robbery and crime;
I shall grant them a sure reward
and make an everlasting covenant
    with them;
their posterity will be renowned among
    the nations
and their descendants among the
    peoples;
all who see them will acknowledge
that they are a race blessed by the
    LORD.
Let me rejoice in the LORD with all my
    heart,

let me exult in my God;
for he has robed me in deliverance
and arrayed me in victory,
like a bridegroom with his garland,
or a bride decked in her jewels.
As the earth puts forth her blossom
or plants in the garden burst into
    flower,
so will the Lord GOD make his victory
    and renown
blossom before all the nations.

Comments on the Story

This passage opens with God speaking. The postexilic prophet puts into the mouth of God powerful words that defend the people of God. Only with data, reflection, and judgment does one realize that these words are not about all the people in the postexilic time. Rather, they witness to the divisions within that community. Indeed, the clearest evidence that these words address a deep community division is verse 7, immediately before our reading. "My people" have suffered abuse and loss, but God will restore their losses "in their own land."

Although the writer is participating in an intracommunity struggle, the modern reader need not know all the specifics of Jewish community life in the fourth century B.C.E. to apply this passage to life today. The Lord's love of justice is indeed something so distinctive to the biblical tradition that one may wonder why this succinct expression of it in verse 8 does not occur elsewhere in the Bible. The pairing of "justice" with "reward" is found in the servant's second song, Isaiah 49:4. The outcry against "robbery and crime" is vague enough that one need not specify an exact reference.

The prophet assures the group that they will have the "everlasting covenant," presumably the one given to the ancestors, not the one made with Israel. The latter covenant had already been broken (Jer. 31:32); the former seemed unbreakable. Just as Second Isaiah called on many resources in the effort to persuade, so also this prophet invokes all traditions that might console and convince.

Exactly who had claim to the special status of "the people of God" was crucial in the postexilic debate. Who are the chosen people of God? For the writer of this passage, clearly the group addressed here has sole right to that claim. The modern reader may prefer to see that those particular promises and privileges are now inherited by all three Abrahamic faiths—Judaism, Christianity, and Islam. These three are now the "race blessed by the Lord" if one must insist on a modern specific for the phrase.

With verse 10 the passage changes tone dramatically. The Lord no longer speaks, but a different voice speaks about God and the action of God.

Many persons today are fond of verse 10 for its use in the Western liturgies on the feast of the Immaculate Conception of the Virgin Mary. This applied sense of the text seems fitting, for the passage emphasizes the deliverance and victory that the speaker receives from God. The joy and exultation redound to the glory of God.

The passage is not clear on the identity of the speaker. The speaker might be the prophet who has received the call to preach fulfillment. Or it might be Zion herself, speaking as she had once spoken so mournfully in Isaiah 49:14. Here she has a cry of joy. One curious element in the speech is the mixed metaphor of double genders, "like a bridegroom . . . or a bride." Zion nowhere else compares herself to a man.

The prophet concludes this passage with metaphors of full assurance that the promise will be fulfilled. Just as the earth is trustworthy in bringing forth her fruits, so also the faithful can trust the God who makes these promises. This prophet, true to the previous borrowing of images from Second Isaiah, here takes as a theme the earth, its sources of energy, its recurrent regeneration, and the inevitability of success (Isa. 55:10-11).

The phrase "before all the nations" is also an example of borrowing. Second Isaiah had the vision and thought of Yahweh's manifestation to the world "before all nations." For this later prophet, the phrase has less force than for Second Isaiah. The words seem to be a quotation that is not fully convincing. One might say that God here uses the weak and less gifted to heal the people and the world. The power of God works even through the limitations of creatures.

Retelling the Story

"God is the gardener. I am only a steward." This is my grandfather's belief. Grandpa says, *"I only plant the seeds. God sends the sun and the rain and the gift of life."* For Grandpa, gardening is a statement of faith.

Grandpa started his backyard garden when he and his family moved into the house near the railroad tracks fifty-one years ago. The dirt was mostly hard, red clay. The summers were hot and dry. The harvest was spare. Grandpa worked the soil with a potato fork and a hand cultivator. He replenished the earth with compost, with straw and manure he hauled from the barns after the state fair was over.

Grandpa is a year-round gardener. He puts his potatoes into the ground in February. He harvests turnips in November. In between the crops of potatoes and turnips, that same soil grows crowder peas. December and January bring time to rest and to order seeds from the seed catalog.

The garden, 50-by-85 feet, takes up the whole backyard. He harvests bushels of vegetables each year. One Christmas, my parents gave him a scale to weigh the produce that would come out of the garden that next year. At the end of the year, the soil had produced a literal ton of food.

Grandma cooks and cans and freezes vegetables and fruit. Whatever is left is shared with neighbors, friends, and strangers. For twelve years, Grandpa has supplied sacks of produce to the church's "Food for Friends" program. The proceeds of the produce sales— $500 a summer—go to hunger ministries. Grandpa used to talk about how hunger could be ended throughout the world if we all were stewards of God's earth.

I remember staying with Grandpa and Grandma during the summer when I was growing up. I learned where to walk and where not to walk in the garden. I helped to look for the squash or tomatoes that were ready to pick. I ran with Grandpa to check the rain gauge after a rain. I sat with Grandpa and Grandma in the backyard as the sun went down and watched the purple martins put on their evening air show.

After I had grown up, I wanted to learn to work in the soil. So I visited Grandpa and followed him around the garden. I listened to his experience and his inspiration. His compost pile

It seems that the rabbi who compared the children of Israel with nuts was not joking. You see, nuts cannot escape being discovered by customs agents because their hard shells rattle against each other as they are carried. Just so, the children of Israel can go nowhere without being recognized. (*Song of Songs Rabbah* 6.11 [1])

As long as the lily can be recognized by its fragrance so will Israel be recognized by its adherence to God's way. And there good deeds will have no end until the fragrance of the lily is gone as well, says one rabbi waxing poetic. (*Song of Songs Rabbah* 2.2 [6]).

was the largest I have ever seen—before or since. All of the grass clippings and leaves from the neighborhood were added to his compost pile. It was almost taller than him—five feet high, eight feet long, and four feet wide. He had a path up to the top of the pile where he would dump the scraps from the kitchen. I was afraid that someday he would fall off that pile and hurt himself. I returned home from that visit, carrying with me a box of vegetables—potatoes, onions, beets, and squash.

When visitors come to see Grandpa, their first stop is the garden to see what is growing. The dirt is no longer red clay. It is dark, rich, fertile soil. It has been fed and loved and cared for by the steward. And it brings forth bounty to feed God's people.

Today I have a garden in my yard. I grow corn, tomatoes, okra, and lots of flowers. When Grandpa visits me, he says, "You can't eat flowers, but they sure are beautiful." That statement is an affirmation of my gardening inheritance. I need to be close to the earth, to put my hands in the dirt, to care for the tender shoots coming forth.

Grandpa, at age eighty-nine, is still gardening. When he was laid up with a back injury, young people came from the church to help work in the garden. His vegetables are still sold on Sunday to raise money for hungry people.

Grandpa's garden continues to spring up from the ground. It is the humble offering of praise from one of God's stewards of the earth. *(Beth Richardson)*

Hephzibah and Beulah

Jerusalem and Zion receive new names as they are married to God.

The Story

For Zion's sake I shall not keep
silent,
for Jerusalem's sake I shall not be
quiet,
until her victory shines forth like the
sunrise,
her deliverance like a blazing torch,
and the nations see your victory
and all their kings your glory.
Then you will be called by a new name
which the LORD himself will
announce;
you will be a glorious crown in the
LORD's hand,
a royal diadem held by your God.
No more will you be called Forsaken,
no more will your land be called
Desolate,
but you will be named Hephzibah
and your land Beulah;
for the LORD will take delight in you
and to him your land will be linked in
wedlock.
As a young man weds a maiden,
so will you be wedded to him who
rebuilds you,
and as a bridegroom rejoices over the
bride,
so will your God rejoice over you.
Jerusalem, on your walls I have posted
watchmen,
who day and night without ceasing will
cry:

'You that invoke the LORD's name,
take no rest, and give no rest to him
until he makes Jerusalem
a theme of praise throughout the
world.'
The LORD has sworn with raised right
hand and mighty arm:
Never again will I give your grain to
feed your foes,
never again let foreigners drink the
vintage
for which you have toiled;
but those who harvest the grain will
eat it
and give praise to the LORD,
and those who gather the grapes will
drink the wine
within my sacred courts.
Pass through the gates, go out,
clear a road for my people;
build a highway, build it up,
remove the boulders;
hoist a signal for the peoples.
This is the LORD's proclamation
to earth's farthest bounds:
Tell the daughter of Zion,
'See, your deliverance comes.
His reward is with him,
his recompense before him.'
They will be called the Holy People,
the Redeemed of the LORD;
and you will be called Sought After,
City No Longer Forsaken.

Comments on the Story

This passage opens with a speaker who is enthusiastic for Zion and her future victorious deliverance. The speaker assures the reader that this future deliverance will be so dramatic that the city will receive a new name, symbolic of her new status.

The speaker is not identified. It might be the prophet, anxious to proclaim the good news of the coming glorification of the city. Probably more likely it is God who speaks, God who had been chided earlier for remaining silent too long.

The victory only awaits God's action. The images of sunrise and a blazing torch are vivid, and they convey the splendor that the prophet foresees for the city. The transformation will be stunning. The nations and kings will all see it, and these great ones will be in awe.

The city becomes a crown. One easily thinks of the Hellenistic coins and artwork that depict city walls as crowns of a deity. The crown that this city is to become will be in the hand of God. If it seems odd that the crown is in the hand and not on the head of God, maybe the reason why is that the image of Yahweh wearing a crown, just like the rival deities, might be inappropriate for the postexilic Jews. Perhaps, too, this imagery that depicts the city as a crown might suggest the idea of the city's being a goddess wearing an ornament to please the city's god. Postexilic thought could not tolerate the existence of more than one deity. Thus the city remains only a crown in the hand of God.

God will award the city with a new name. The changing of names in Israelite culture signals a new status or role for the person whose name is changed. This city will receive directly from God a completely new name.

Repeatedly in the prophetic literature Jerusalem is told that she will get a new name. And the prophets seem determined to change her name. A probable reason is that the name she has had, appearing first in Egyptian documents of the nineteenth century B.C.E., carries within itself the name of a Canaanite god. ("Foundation of Shalim" is a possible translation of the ancient city name "Jerusalem.")

The prophets seem determined also to rid the city of the evidence of a different god. Here the prophet proposes the names "Hephzibah" ("My delight is in her") and, for her land, "Beulah" (meaning "married"). Both titles suggest the sexual imagery of a Canaanite god and the city in which he resides. In our passage, both the city and the land belonging to it would be seen as companions to the god.

The name "Hephzibah" has a parallel construction with the names that Ezekiel gives Samaria and Jerusalem in Ezekiel 23. These names are Oholah ("her tent"/"she who has a tent"), for Samaria, and Oholibah ("my tent is in her"), for Jerusalem. Ezekiel portrays both cities as wives of God. But the book

116

of Isaiah names only Jerusalem as God's wife, and here Zion's land seems also to be married to God.

The marriage imagery that the prophet uses in verse 5 has been restored by the REB. The Hebrew text that survives actually reads "your sons will marry you." However, most modern translations see that this as an error in the vocalization of the Hebrew text. The NRSV, changing no consonants but only the vowel signs, reads: "your builder shall marry you."

The normal relation between a husband and wife in the Hebrew Bible seems to be evident here (and we find comparable passages in other parts of the Bible). That relation is characterized by joy. Even though the Bible comes to us from a clearly patriarchal society, the marital love that couples shared was true and joyful and enjoyable. God's joy for the beloved city may be compared to that kind of love.

The mention of the city walls has been a focus of commentators. Postexilic Jerusalem's walls were not fully rebuilt until probably about 450, more than seventy years after the return of the first Jews from Babylon. Hence, it is unclear whether the watchmen posted on the walls are meant literally or are in the realm of the author's imagination. More important is the spirit they seem to instill in the people. One after another, people join in the recognition of Jerusalem and of the city's status. Ultimately Jerusalem becomes known and honored by the whole world.

The view shifts suddenly in verses 8-9 from the expansive and elevated ideas of worldwide praise for Jerusalem to the matter of the Jews in Judea eating their own produce. In earlier times, others had profited from the workers' labor. In the fulfilled times, the products and harvests will be the people's own. This verse may refer to the competition and hostility between the returned exiles and those who had remained in the land during the exile.

The last three verses, 10-12, are made up, for the most part, of quoted phrases from Second Isaiah. One can see the importance that certain Jews gave to the words of that exilic prophet. It was important to reassure the people of the earlier promises. The people would indeed and without doubt be the redeemed, holy people. The city that had been neglected and divorced most definitively would be called "Sought After," "City No Longer Forsaken."

Retelling the Story

> No more will you be called Forsaken.
> Isaiah 62:4

My name was Desolate, Forsaken, Despised.

Father was a drinker. When he drank, he wasn't much of a father. He hit my mother and my older brothers, but he didn't hit me. He came to me in the night and loved on me. That was what he called it. He didn't hit me, but he forced me.

That happened as far back as I can remember—not that I can remember much from my childhood. It's like one of those scenes you see at the theater, where a pretty picture is painted on a fabric screen. But then they bring up the lights behind the screen and you see a horrible sight—people beat up and bleeding and moaning.

> It was God's great love for Israel, according to the sages, that set guards on the parapets of the world to watch over God's beloved people. (*Exodus Rabbah* 18.5)

My family looked liked that—all nice and perfect on the outside. But behind the pretty picture was drinking and disaster.

Today I look at the photographs from when I was little. The face is smiling, but the eyes are vacant. The pictures are of a little girl I do not know, toys I do not remember, places I've never seen. I know the pictures are of me, but I cannot remember that little girl.

I left home as soon as I turned eighteen and married the first guy who asked me. He was nice enough, but he hit me like my father hit my mother. I swore that I'd never drink, but I had to do something for the pain and the loneliness.

Next thing I knew, I was thirty years old. I have a second husband and three kids. I'm in a detox center. My family put me there. I'm hurting and shaking, and I wish I would just die. My life has never been worth anything. I was damaged goods by the time I was six. If I could get enough pills, I would stop things right now. But, damn it, there are no pills, no death, no easy way out. The only way out is to get clean.

As soon as I got sober, the nightmares started. I woke up screaming in the night, afraid of my father. The doctors said I had post-traumatic stress syndrome, just like the Vietnam vets. For me there were no helicopters, only the memory of a big, silent, stinking man on top of me.

> Some sages say the removal of boulders from God's highway represented the removal of evil impulses from the lives of God's people. God promised that if we would remove some of these impulses in this life that in the world to come the rest would disappear from our way. (*Numbers Rabbah* 15.16)

My kids and my husband tried to understand. He would hold me when I was afraid, if I would let him. The kids just loved me the way kids do. I cried when I watched them, thinking about what I had gone through at their age. How could anyone be so cruel?

I went to a therapist to help me with the nightmares. I was finally able to see the scene of destruction that hid behind the perfect facade. I was, for the first time, able to feel the terror and the grief and the shame that I could not feel as a little girl. The pain of the remembering was as vivid as if it had happened yesterday.

I felt desolate, forsaken, despised, full of shame. My therapist told me that I would have to be loved into being. And that's what she did—and my husband and my children—they loved me into being. They believed in me and loved me no matter what had happened to me. When I felt totally depressed and unlovable, they still loved me.

Slowly I began to be. I felt more like me than ever in my life. Before, I related to the world through layers—of fear, shame, addiction, depression. I started to lose the layers one by one, and I stood before the world fresh and new. I felt vulnerable, tender, and a little bit shaky. But I was shored up with love.

It was sort of like getting a new me—like becoming the person that my higher power meant me to be. I am no longer named Despised and Wounded. My new name is One Who Was Broken, but Now Is Whole. My higher power calls me Sought Out, because I was lost, and now I'm found. I am Mother, Spouse, Woman, Child of God. I was called Forsaken, but now I am called Loved. I am living for the very first time. *(Beth Richardson)*

A Disappointed Parent

God wonders if his children will be true to their potential.

The Story

I shall recount the LORD's unfailing love,
the prowess of the LORD,
according to all he has done for us,
his great goodness to the house of Israel,
what he has done for them in his tenderness
and by his many acts of faithful love.
He said, 'Surely they are my people,
children who will not play me false';
and he became their deliverer
in all their troubles.
No envoy, no angel, but he himself delivered them,
redeemed them in his love and pity;
he lifted them up and carried them
through all the days of old.

Comments on the Story

This reading consists of only the opening three verses of a long passage in the form of the communal laments that we find in the Psalms. This kind of formal service has certain traditional parts, all of which appear here: the remembrance of God's gracious acts of old (63:7-14), a plea with a depiction of the people's current plight (63:15–64:5a), a confession of sins (64:5b-7), and finally a concluding appeal (64:8-12). A few of the ideas appear in more than one part.

The hymn starts out in the first-person singular, as in many such laments. An individual, as spokesperson for the group, sings of the graciousness of God as revealed in the many kind deeds God has done in the past. The ingenuity of God's love in leading Israel on its way shines out in the actions done on their behalf.

The mention of "the house of Israel" probably is not intended to refer to the Northern Kingdom that had split off from the Davidic rule in Jerusalem. Rather, the reference is to the great story of Israel. Second Isaiah had referred to Abraham, and this lament will mention him in 64:16, but in an ambiguous way. So this prophet wants his readers to think of Israel's story as including the traditional ancestors.

The expression "they are my people" suggests the covenant made at Sinai. This agreement on the part of Israel and Yahweh that they would be mutually bound to each other is powerful motivation and background for the lament that follows.

God begins the reflection with the supposed thought that the people would be true and not "play me false." Perhaps this is the hope of every parent in every age. Children come so small and dependent on their parents that the parents have a long time to ponder the probability of the child's remaining true to them. Yahweh is depicted as thinking aloud and with the hope that Israel will reflect on the deeds done for them. Reality catches up with this (metaphorical) father, and he will experience the disappointments that most parents eventually endure.

God's role as deliverer in verses 8c-9a seems to include episodes occurring before the Sinai encounter. Both on the earliest stages and in the later, more historical, periods, Israel experienced God's willingness and actual activity to save the people from the difficulties they experience and opponents who work against them.

Quite remarkable is the insistence on God's doing the saving without the use of any other figure. God could not just be an observer, a boss who could send an assistant to take care of the matter. Sometimes even in major crises, the boss can't come but sends a substitute. Here, however, the claim is that God doesn't work that way. When God is needed, when there is a need, God comes.

"No envoy, no angel" actually does not sound like some of the texts that appear elsewhere in the Bible. Both envoys and messengers abound in the biblical texts. The diversity of substitutes in the biblical tradition is quite broad, beginning with the guards God puts at the garden to block entrance (Gen. 3:24) to the mysterious extra figure in the fiery furnace in Daniel 3:25.

Yet there are many texts in which the divine initiative and direct action are equally emphasized. God does not always wait until asked. God needed no one to suggest that Abraham be chosen and sent on his pilgrimage. God sometimes just butts in, as it were, when there is a problem.

The picture of God lifting the people up and personally carrying them fits in well with the depiction of God as shepherd in Second Isaiah (40:11). The reading leaves us with the thought that God's love and pity take care of Israel "through all the days of old." Israel seems to be at a turning point in its history. The people have returned to Jerusalem, and things are underway to move on in its life's story. The storyteller might think of a young person at a critical time in the period of maturation. What does the future hold? What am I to do to walk and live with God?

Retelling the Story

The people were gathered around her. She was a diminutive woman, dressed in a brown suit, her gray hair neatly styled. All around them were display cases and large, brightly illuminated screens telling the story of the Holocaust. Crowds of people silently filed past the screens, reading and looking at the pictures. No one thought that the Anne Frank exhibit would touch the souls of so many people. But the people came, day after day. People of all ages came to see and to pay tribute to the life of Anne Frank and the millions of others who had died.

The display cases were filled with artifacts—a yellow fabric star of David, a child's shoes. And grotesque Nazi memorabilia—a desecrated scroll, items made from human hair.

In the middle of the pictures, artifacts, and crowds of people sat the woman, a survivor of the death camps. People gathered around to listen as she told stories and answered questions. She looked like an ordinary woman, perhaps someone's grandmother. Her face reflected neither bitterness nor hatred. Anyone searching her eyes for some sign of all the horrors that she had experienced would find only a depth that reflected one's own questioning, one's own agony and grief.

She was a child—ten years old—when her family was transported to the concentration camp. She was the only survivor of her immediate family. When the Allies freed her camp, she was thirteen. She had managed to survive for three years in hell.

She told about daily life in the camps. One could almost imagine sitting and listening to a grandparent who was relating stories about life on the farm. But the stories were about daily life in a concentration camp. She spoke with calmness and honesty.

Someone asked whether it was difficult for her to talk about the experience. She said that, yes, it was difficult. But it was important for her to be here so that all could hear the truth. Only by keeping the memory alive could the world be saved from falling again into such evil.

> The rabbis say that when God's people suffer, God suffers. That is the reason God called to Moses from a thornbush. Can you think of a less comfortable place from which to speak? Even as God heard the cries of the slaves in Egypt, God also shared their plan. (*Exodus Rabbah* 2.5)

Someone asked her about whether she had faith in God. She paused and then nodded yes. She said that she has faith in God, that sometimes she has to reach back to the stories of the ancestors—to the courage of Abraham and Sarah, Isaac and Rebekah, Joseph, Esther, and Ruth. She had to remember the gracious deeds of the Lord, who brought the people out of Egyptian slavery into the promised land.

Even so, she said, it is difficult to understand the suffering. There are no easy answers to the questions. But most of the time, she believes that the faithfulness and mercy of God have continued despite the attempts of human beings to overcome goodness with evil. So many died, not on account of God, but at the hands of human beings. God was present with them in the suffering and with each soul who perished.

Tears were in all eyes as her listeners stood there. She sat silently for a while. Then she continued, "When I was in the camp, sometimes I thought I saw an angel. It wasn't a person, I'm sure. When I saw it, it glowed with brilliant light, just for a second. When I was afraid, I thought of that light. It always gave me a feeling that I wasn't alone. To this day, I don't know what it was. Maybe it was God's presence there ministering to us, the ones who lived and the ones who died."

She told us to keep hoping and praying and working for the good. And she asked God to bless each of us.

We began to disperse. Many wanted to thank her, to touch her. It was difficult to leave her presence. When I finally left, I felt that I had been in the presence of someone who was close to God. I felt that God's love had touched me through her. *(Beth Richardson)*

The Children Appeal

The children of Israel appeal to God the Father to reappear as he did among their ancestors.

The Story

Why did you not tear asunder
the heavens and come down,
that, when you appeared, the
mountains might shake,
that fire might blaze as it blazes in
brushwood
when it makes water boil?
Then would your name be known to
your adversaries,
and nations would tremble before you.
You surprised us with awesome things;
the mountains shook when you
appeared.
Never has ear heard or eye seen
any other god who acts for those who
wait for him.
You welcome him who rejoices to do
what is right,
who is mindful of your ways.
When you showed your anger, we
sinned

and, in spite of it, we have done evil
from of old.
We all became like something unclean
and all our righteous deeds were like a
filthy rag;
we have all withered like leaves
and our iniquities carry us away like
the wind.
There is no one who invokes you by
name
or rouses himself to hold fast to you;
for you have hidden your face from us
and left us in the grip of our
iniquities.
Yet, LORD, you are our Father;
we are the clay, you the potter,
and all of us are your handiwork.
Do not let your anger pass all bounds,
LORD,
and do not remember iniquity for ever;
look on us all, look on your people.

Comments on the Story

Bible translations differ in interpreting the first verse of this reading. (Some differ over whether the first line should be 64:1*a*, as in the REB and the NRSV, or 63:19*b*, as in the Hebrew text, which the New Jerusalem Bible follows.) The NRSV translates the verse as a prayer for immediate divine intervention. The REB reads it as part of the cause of the present condition of the people: God has not intervened.

One can agree with the NRSV and see the plea for some dramatic intervention in history. The tearing asunder of the heavens for God to descend is certainly a striking image. The quaking of the mountains at the appearance of God is a vivid element in the exodus narrative. But the exodus does not include the tearing of the sky. For modern people, the sky can hardly be torn. But for the ancients, the sky was like a bowl put over the (flat) earth. Within that perspective, this passage is less problematic. In this interpretation of the verse, the author pleads with God to reveal the divine might as was done in the past. Included here seem to be the fire of the burning bush and the revelation of God's special name, Yahweh, from the book of Exodus. With such an old-style divine action, the people could find some success.

But one can, alternatively, agree with the REB in its understanding of the verse and see this action as something that God could have done but didn't. The author simply mentions the thought that God could have acted in a dazzling way, the way of divine action in the distant past, and such a display might have stopped Israel from going in the wrong path. God could have "surprised us" as in the past. But God didn't make a such show, and Israel sinned.

The author has a brief reflection on the nature of God as perceived by Israel. Israel's God was always depicted as acting in wondrous ways toward the elect people. The author exaggerates the distinctiveness of this Israelite experience over against the ancient Near East in general. "Never has ear heard or eye seen" such a god. Yet the texts from the time show us various gods doing comparable things. Israel's experience of God did go beyond the idea here of a God who acts in history to that of a God of self-giving love.

It is, perhaps, with this thought in mind that Paul quoted this passage (but clearly from a text worded quite differently from what we now have) in 1 Corinthians 2:9. Paul is applying the verse to the experience of God and the wisdom of God that so contradicts the boastful claims of haughty human beings. God prepares surprises for those who share love.

The author ends this section on the state of the people by noting (v. 5a) that God looks for people who delight in the ways of God and who act according to the way God acts. God hopes for people of good will. All depends on the encounter between the human and the divine.

A confession of sin begins in the second half of verse 5. (The NRSV appropriately marks the shift with a "but.") Not only have the people sinned, but also they have "done evil from of old." Even when God warned them, they sinned. The writer suggests that the miserable condition in which the people now find themselves has been brought on by them. This thought recurs in the biblical tradition with uncomfortable frequency.

The problem with sin, this text avers, is that it drives God and people further apart. The images used are alarming. "Something unclean" would be anything that might render a person ritually unfit to enter the Temple, the house of God. "A filthy rag" refers to cloth used by a woman in menstruation, an object that would render anyone temporarily unable to enter the holy place.

The images of the withered leaves and windblown objects portray the instability of one without God. Much worse is the action of God. "You have hidden your face from us." God has abandoned the people to their sins and the consequences of those sins. No wonder that a plea rises up to God.

The plea begins with images that are bound to win the favor and mercy of God. God is invoked as Father, recalling probably the first (Exod. 4:4) and most enduring of the images employed to describe the relation between God and Israel. Fatherhood can vary perhaps as much as do fathers. A common theme would be responsibility and affection. Does God really want the son (the people Israel), the children (the Jews) whom God begot, simply to become lost and unfulfilled?

The author is not satisfied with the image of paternity. God is also depicted as an artisan (as in Genesis 2) who had crafted this people. Can either a father or an artist give up on what he had started? Surely, the author thinks, God will follow through on this project of humanity.

Retelling the Story

Some say that before the earth was formed there was a tree of life and that all was created from that tree. Others say that an old turtle swam to the bottom of the ocean and brought up the mud from which the earth was fashioned. Some people say creation was made from chaos or from nothing or from sacrifice. Some recall that the earth was flung into the darkness by a divine being-creator. Whatever the name—Creator, Father, Great Spirit, Allah, Yahweh—and in whatever fashion, God created the earth, the universe, and all that exists.

God created this planet with all its creatures. We human beings are one of the creatures. We have been blessed with the gifts of the earth—food, shelter, clothing—abundant blessings. We have tilled the land, conquered the forces of nature. We have used the earth's resources to meet our human needs.

At the same time, we have received the responsibility to care for the earth—for the land, the water, the air, the animals, the birds, the vegetation. We are stewards of God's creation.

What does the Creator God think of us human creatures? We have not respected our earth. We have pushed the earth's abundance and resources to the limits. And now the delicate balance of life on earth has been disturbed. This has happened only

These were differing opinions among the rabbis concerning what the eye has not seen. One said it referred to the Messianic age, another suggested that it was the world to come, while still a third said it was Eden. Since no human eye (at least none since our first forebears left the garden) has seen any of these, they could all be right. (*Sefer Ha-Aggadah* 399.1)

recently, though we like to think that it began millions of years ago when the dinosaurs disappeared.

Animals, birds, and plants are dying, becoming extinct. The air and water are polluted by human endeavors. In some places, the land has been irrevocably altered, so that no life can survive on it. Even the atmosphere of the earth, the place where the earth and the universe meet, has been compromised.

From space, the earth is a green and blue marble hanging on black velvet. From space, they say, the earth looks like the fragile place that it is.

As human beings, may we cry to God for mercy.

We have been greedy in our human endeavors, raping the earth's resources to meet our needs, not regarding the consequences of our behavior.

Forgive us, creating God.

We have failed to live in harmony with our neighbors—the deer and the elephant, the eagle and the whale. We have taken from the generous bounty of the earth without giving back its resources.

Forgive us, creating God.

We have poisoned the very air that we need to live. We have polluted the water that we drink. We have set priorities that foster death over life.

Forgive us, creating God.

Another two sages disagreed about whom God will welcome home. One said that it would first be those who were completely righteous. But another said that even the totally righteous could not replace in God's heart those who had come back through repentance. (*Sefer Ha-Aggadah* 506.225)

Have mercy on us, creating God. You shaped the world and all that is in it. Do not destroy the earth because of the foolishness of your human children. Do not throw us away like a broken pot. Mend our brokenness. Shape us, Potter God, like the clay you formed into the new earth.

Have mercy, creating God, on your children and on your earth. *(Beth Richardson)*

The Disappointed Parent Responds

God advises disobedient children that God is easily found, but they prefer to pursue repulsive rituals.

The Story

I was ready to respond, but no one asked,
ready to be found, but no one sought me,
I said, 'Here am I! Here am I!'
to a nation that did not invoke me by name.
All day long I held out my hands
appealing to a rebellious people
who went their evil way,
in pursuit of their own devices;
they were a people who provoked me
perpetually to my face,
offering sacrifice in the gardens,
burning incense on brick altars.
They crouch among graves,
keeping vigil all night long,
eating the flesh of pigs,
their cauldrons full of a foul brew.
'Keep clear!' they cry,
'Do not touch me, for my holiness will infect you.'
Such people are a smouldering fire,
smoke in my nostrils all day long.

Your record lies before me; I shall not keep silent;
I shall fully repay your iniquities,
both yours and your forefathers', says the LORD,
for having sacrificed on the mountains
and shamed me on the hills;
I shall first measure out their reward
and then repay them in full.
These are the words of the LORD:
As there is juice in a cluster of grapes
and folk say, 'Do not destroy it; there is blessing in it,'
so shall I act for the sake of my servants:
I shall not destroy the whole nation.
I shall give descendants to Jacob,
and to Judah heirs who will possess my mountains;
my chosen ones will take possession of the land,
and those who serve me will live there.

Comments on the Story

The speaker throughout this passage is God. It has two sections: Verses 1-7 are an accusation against a group of people who are not faithful to God, and verses 8-9 are a promise of reward for "the chosen ones" to whom is promised possession of the land. The passage is a clear witness to the tensions within the postexilic community and to the variety of new intellectual developments in that time.

The plaintive cry put on the lips of God is moving. God wants people to

129

worship rightly; God is willing to be won over by good will. This winning should be easy for those who know what pleases God. At stake here is approaching God with seriousness and with full devotion. God stands ready and uses the same words that humans say when God calls to them, "Here am I! Here am I!"

Paul quotes verse 1 in his Letter to the Romans (10:20-21). He reads these verses as if they were a critique of the whole nation. But the analysis of the later verses indicates that it is not the whole nation that is being reprimanded. Rather, the specific division within the community allows the reproach to be specified. Those in power, returning to Jerusalem under funding from the Persian government, have excluded those who had never left the land.

The specific description in the passage may refer either to people who practice rituals not directed to Yahweh, the God of Israel, or to those Israelites who worship in the holy place of that God but who do not do justice to other human beings. Details in the text indicate that the latter group, those priests who benefited from the Persian-sponsored return, are the persons being attacked.

The choice of practices that are condemned in the dominant class in the society may seem almost harmless. Probably all of them—"offering sacrifice in the gardens,/burning incense on brick altars./They crouch among graves,/keeping vigil all night long,/eating the flesh of pigs"—are meant to be symbolic of the worst that this author could think of at the time. Some of these rituals were ancient Cannanite practices, while others are rites prohibited by the Mosaic Law.

"Keep clear! Do not touch me, for my holiness will infect you." This supposed cry of such people does accurately reflect the idea that there are degrees of ritual holiness and that one must not enter the holy places that have special degrees of holiness too quickly and without the needed ritual purification.

God is depicted as saying that such behavior puts a person at risk. God will repay all injustices: those that offend the divine holiness and those that offend human beings. God is said to be moved by such behavior. God is especially moved because these people, by doing shameful deeds, have rejected the invitation that God had so openly and freely offered. These people are following the example set by the ancestors (the writer assumes), and they will receive just judgment and punishment.

But the story does not end there. God is not going to wipe out the people, for there are some friends of God among those wicked ones. Just as one wouldn't throw out bushels of apples because there are a few bad ones among the good, so also God is not going to destroy the whole nation. (Note how the phrase "a people" in vv. 2-3 does not refer to the entirety of the Jews of the postexilic community.) The few "servants" of the Lord will be saved by that Lord.

We see in this passage the seeds of the idea of a final, universal judgment. One notes, too, in verse 6 a reference to "your record." The idea of a book that records all one's deeds is beginning to gain currency in this period of Israel's history.

Another idea gaining ground in the popular mentality of the time is the significant weight of one's own actions for the individual's future life. In earlier times there was a heavy emphasis on the people as a whole. A remnant of the nation (not the individual) would be saved; now the focus is on the individual. It may well be that "my servants" is an organized sect within the Jews of that time. This author seems to limit salvation to those few.

The final promise is possession, ownership of the land. This hope is presented as the primordial promise to the ancestors. But in reality the promise could well be a late projection back to an earlier time. Those excluded from power are using this theme here against those who now have control of the land and power.

And the other aspects of the ancestral promises are here too. That promise included the idea of many descendants; it included the pledge of a special relationship. To be God's own people is clearly the claim of the group.

The storyteller might focus on the disappointed God; a God who had hoped to be properly received is rejected by some. Another option is the idea of a blessing repeated in a new setting, in the mid–postexilic community.

Retelling the Story

> I was ready to respond, but no one asked,
> ready to be found, but no one sought me.
> I said, 'Here am I! Here am I!'
> Isaiah 65:1

I don't seek pity. I look not for guilt or remorse or excuses. What I want from you, my children, is faithfulness, responsiveness. I have held out my hands to you ever since I created you. But you have ignored me, shunned me, disobeyed me.

I am not angry. I am sad and lonely. I yearn for you, for your partnership with me. I hunger for your participation in the covenant that I made with your ancestors.

I created you in the beginning and asked only that you eat not from the tree of the knowledge of good and evil. But you did not follow my desires. So you were sent away from the garden.

I tried to teach you my ways, but you followed all sorts of evil. I was angry and disappointed at how you had become. In my anger, I sent the flood and destroyed much of what I had created. But I was sorry about what I had done, and I made a covenant with you never again to destroy creation.

I offered the covenant to your ancestors, to Abraham and Sarah. I blessed them with descendants. I walked with your forebears through wars and famines and slavery.

When you were slaves in Egypt, I sent Moses to lead you out of bondage. I performed great deeds that overcame your captors. I brought you out of Egypt, even as you were pursued by the soldiers. I led you through the wilderness. I fed you and cared for you even when you complained mightily.

Although you were a stiff-necked people, I pardoned every iniquity. At Mount Sinai, I gave you my commandments and made with you an everlasting covenant, "keeping steadfast love for the thousandth generation" (Exod. 34:7 NRSV). You shall be my people, and I shall be your God.

That covenant has been broken many times by you. But I have remained steadfast and faithful. I continue to call you back to me.

I have watched with pain as, through the centuries, you have fought one another in my name. You have continued to be a stiff-necked, selfish people, believing that only your way is the right way, condemning your brothers and sisters for seeing me differently. You have damaged my creation—the land, the air, the birds, animals, and fish, which I created. You have acted as if you were the only inhabitants on earth, that you, alone, were to be cared for and honored. I am sad and lonely and disappointed with you, my people. When will you learn? When will you remember whose you are and return to me?

The ones who are faithful to me are few in number. Your voices cry out like the wind across a desert. Few people hear your pleas, your prophecy, your call to accountability.

For the sake of you, faithful servants, I will not destroy them all.

You who hear this, listen and come. I am waiting to be found by you. I hold out my hands. Come to me. I wait for you with love and forgiveness, mercy and reconciliation. I yearn for you, my people. Seek me, for I am here. *(Beth Richardson)*

One sage interpreted the blessing in the cluster of grapes as meaning that a blessing should be spoken over it. One pious vineyard keeper went into the vineyard on the Sabbath, found a ripe cluster, and said a blessing over it, though he was forbidden to pick it on the Sabbath. Thus we can say a blessing over that which we will not see harvested. (*Genesis Rabbah* 29.2)

The Fulfilled Jerusalem

God will create something so new that all suffering and premature death will disappear so that fruitful work and fulfilling love are enjoyed.

The Story

See, I am creating new heavens and
     a new earth!
The past will no more be remembered
nor will it ever come to mind.
Rejoice and be for ever filled with
     delight
at what I create;
for I am creating Jerusalem as a
     delight
and her people as a joy;
I shall take delight in Jerusalem
and rejoice in my people;
the sound of weeping, the cry of
     distress
will be heard in her no more.
No child there will ever again die in
     infancy,
no old man fail to live out his span of
     life.
He who dies at a hundred is just a
     youth,
and if he does not attain a hundred he
     is thought accursed!
My people will build houses and live
     in them,
plant vineyards and eat their fruit;
they will not build for others to live in
or plant for others to eat.
They will be as long-lived as a tree,
and my chosen ones will enjoy the
     fruit of their labour.
They will not toil to no purpose
or raise children for misfortune,
because they and their issue after
     them
are a race blessed by the LORD.
Even before they call to me, I shall
     answer,
and while they are still speaking I
     shall respond.
The wolf and the lamb will feed
     together
and the lion will eat straw like the ox,
and as for the serpent, its food will be
     dust.
Neither hurt nor harm will be done in
     all my holy mountain,
says the LORD.

Comments on the Story

This passage has an opening verse that seems not to fit too well with the rest of the passage. The promise of a new heaven and a new earth would be more appropriate if some description of that new heaven and earth followed. Instead, the focus is on the re-creation of the city of Jerusalem and on the fulfillment of the people in it. The writer's thoughts center on the city that is featured so prominently in Isaiah 40–66.

The period of this re-creation will be a time of utter completeness of all that is incomplete and a fulfillment of all human hopes. The writer takes pains to find the right ideas and the right expression for this wondrous time. Some of the writer's difficulties come out in the unusual Hebrew expressions used (but the REB smooths out those awkward parts).

The first way of showing this fulfillment is the contrast between joy and sorrow. Life is universally recognized as a vale of tears, an existence of suffering. But this writer predicts that the sound of weeping will no longer be heard. No doubt, the writer meant that there will be no more reason for weeping to occur.

Sometimes death represents the ultimate in suffering, whether in the individual or in her or his survivors. This passage takes up the universal human problem of death as a major focus. Probably the most disturbing of deaths is that of an infant. The writer says simply that infant death will not occur in that time. Moreover, ordinary persons will live out their expected lifetimes. The surprising thing here is that for the ordinary person, a lifetime is seen as a hundred years. This is quite unusual for the Bible. Psalm 90:10 regards seventy years as a normal lifespan, if indeed one succeeds in living that long.

Death will take no one by surprise. All will receive their allotted times. Life is to be lived as long as it is here, and it will not be foreshortened in its time. The writer never seems to have considered that death might be conquered, as it is said to be in a later text (Isa. 25:8; some would say that death is not conquered until the resurrection of Jesus).

The promise is given that there will never be another invasion of the land by hostile enemies. The promise is couched in terms of the people's not losing their houses or vineyards. Their houses will remain right there to live in. Their vineyards will again offer them their fruit.

As a tree grows, so will the people grow and flourish in the time of fulfillment. Note how that time is not depicted as a time of idleness or simply of barren relaxation. Rather, the fulfilled person is one whose work is not thwarted of its activity and fruition.

The two ideas in verse 23a almost parallel the famous saying of Freud: "To work and to love." In the time of fulfillment neither work nor childrearing will ever be frustrated. Both activities can lead to failure and frustration, but in that time, labor in general and being a parent in particular will not be in vain.

Most of chapter 65 has an identifiable emphasis on individuality, but there is none here. Rather, the lead goes in the direction of communality in the statement that Israel is a blessed race (v. 23d). The people are seen as a whole. (Perhaps it should be pointed out that there is no word for "race" in Hebrew.)

Verse 24 contains an incredible promise: "Even before they call to me, I shall answer,/ and while they are still speaking I shall respond." Nothing can compare to the depiction of God's eagerness to help the creature that God has made (the thought parallels Isa. 65:1). No need goes unattended, because God is standing ready, waiting for the chance to care for humans.

The writer, or a later scribe, is moved in another direction by the thought of this time of fulfillment. The passage from Isaiah 11:6-9 came to mind. That passage clearly looks for a time when all would be different from the present world. All antipathies will disappear. The experience of peace will be universal. This writer endorses that vision wholeheartedly. All the ancient conflicts will be gone. Peace universal will reign.

In a surprise reference, perhaps, the writer pulls in what must have seemed the most ancient antagonism, that between humans and serpents, one that appears already in Genesis 3:14. Even that struggle will be over.

The passage closes with the claim that this peace will emanate from "My holy mountain." Jerusalem will stand at the end, but this time the city will be the fulfilled Jerusalem.

Retelling the Story

No child there will ever again die in infancy.
(Isa. 65:20)

He was born HIV positive. His mother didn't know she had HIV until she went for prenatal care. He has an older sister who is three. She doesn't know or understand what's ahead—the loss of her mother and her brother to HIV/AIDS.

Today he is going to be baptized. The congregation sings, "Help us accept each other as Christ accepted us. Teach us, as sister, brother, each person to embrace." As they sing, he is carried to the center of the congregation. He is small for a two-year-old. He has curly blond hair. He is quiet and still. They must cradle him like an infant, supporting his head. A feeding tube is taped to his face. His eyes look deep, fragile, wise.

The pastor says that today Terry is brought for baptism by his adopted fathers, Dennis and Tom. Standing between Dennis and Tom is Linda, Terry's mother. Curly-headed Sarah,

> The tree mentioned in verse 22 is Torah according to certain sages. They say that the Torah will endure forever since it was created for Israel's sake. And Israel will endure because it was created for its own sake. (*Ecclesiastes Rabbah* 1.4 [4])

> Of the many things that will be different in the world to come is that there will be no crying or weeping. All sorrow will end, the rabbis say, since death will be no more. (*Exodus Rabbah* 15.2)

Terry's sister, is held by Tom. Linda has given up custody of the children so that no matter what happens to her, they will be loved and cared for. She visits them every day, hoping that the children will have some memory of her when she is gone.

The pastor speaks to the congregation: "We are going to baptize Terry today. Terry has HIV/AIDS. Dennis and Tom want him to be baptized now, because Terry may not live much longer. As a congregation, we have two choices. We can become paralyzed by the grief of this moment, or we can celebrate the promise of life and new creation inherent in this sacrament."

The congregation opens their hymnals to the service of baptism for infants. All three adults affirm their commitments to care for the faith life of Terry. The congregation promises to surround Terry with a community of love and forgiveness, to pray for him, to live in the example of Christ. In the face of certain death, the community affirms the richness of Terry's life as a child of God.

And then the pastor holds the baby in his arms, takes water and places it on Terry's head, and says the ancient words, "Terry Wayne, I baptize you in the name of the Father and of the Son and of the Holy Spirit."

Terry utters not a sound. His daddy Dennis carries him up the aisle of the church so that he can see his new community, his new family. The congregation sings, "Bless his life, Lord. Come by here. Oh, Lord, come by here."

Dennis and Tom talk about the significance of this event for them. Tom introduces one of his grown sons and says that he never expected to raise another family. He says that people ask them, "How can you do this—take an HIV/AIDS baby?" And he answers them, "How can we *not* do this? Terry has brought to our lives such great joy and happiness."

The room is alive with love. It is alive with grief and hope and courage. You can see it in the people's faces, in their moist eyes and cheeks. The people are witnesses to God's new creation. It is a place where family expands beyond kinship, where hope outlives despair, where faith and love conquer death. A little child leads them to God's presence.

Terry's life, however short it may be, is made rich and full in the love and grace of God. *(Beth Richardson)*

ISAIAH 66:10-14

A Mother Surprised by a Sudden Birth

A mother's milk gives comfort to those who love her.

The Story

Rejoice with Jerusalem and exult in
    her,
all you that love her;
share her joy with all your heart,
all you that mourned over her.
Then you may suck comfort from her
    and be satisfied,
taking with enjoyment her plentiful
    milk.
These are the words of the LORD:
I shall make prosperity flow over her
    like a river,

and the wealth of nations like a
    stream in spate;
her babes will be carried in her arms
and dandled on her knees.
As a mother comforts her son
so shall I myself comfort you;
in Jerusalem you will find comfort.
At the sight your heart will be glad,
you will flourish like grass in spring;
the LORD will make his power known
    among his servants
and his indignation felt among his
    foes.

Comments on the Story

This passage was originally intended to give consolation to those who had returned from exile. It speaks admirably of the abundant gifts that God promises to the faithful ones. The rich, lush, and sensual tones of the picture described must be attractive to any sensitive human being. This consolation certainly must have been attractive to the people of the fifth or fourth century B.C.E. The prophet knew the depths of the human heart and did not hesitate to call upon those depths.

The call to rejoice with Jerusalem implies that the reader knows that Jerusalem is already rejoicing. The reason for her rejoicing in this passage is found in verses 7-9, the sudden birth of her children without any period of gestation or labor. The careful reader notices that the prophetic metaphor of Zion as a mother differs in use between Second and Third Isaiah. Second Isaiah (49:18-23; 54:1-3) has Zion being surprised by having children she didn't know she had, who now are coming from a distance to her. Here the different idea of a sudden birth might catch one by surprise.

The writer moves from the idea of a sudden birth to the image of a nursing mother. Jerusalem will share her joy and her strength as a mother shares with

137

her nursing infant. Even those who had mourned in the loss of status for the city and the loss of freedom for her citizens now can rejoice in the abundance of consolation the city offers.

The picture of a river in the city takes us momentarily away from the depiction of the city as a woman. Third Isaiah is not alone in using the image of a river in connection with the fulfilled Zion (see Ps. 46:4; Ezek. 47:1; Zech. 14:8).

The notion of God as a mother (v. 13) is quite effective. This comparison is rarely made in the Hebrew Bible. Of the few times that it occurs, the greatest concentration is in Isaiah 40–66. This comparison of God with a mother may have been made easy for the prophets who wrote these chapters because of the frequent depiction of Zion as a mother in this material.

The portrayals of the mother's carrying her child at the breast and bouncing the child on her knees form a delightful picture. At first the reader is not sure whether the mother is Zion or God. But the author clarifies the point with the words "as a mother ... so shall I myself. ... " The author, it can be noted, does not say that God is female. This text does, however, freely and delightfully give God traits and activities that are traditionally those of a woman. The Bible never says that God is male or female, but its traditions and writers offer various images for God, some that are male and some that are female. The grammatical gender of God (masculine), nevertheless, does not change.

The reading ends before the traditional end of the verse in Hebrew. The clause that it omits at the end is "and his indignation [is] felt among his foes." No doubt there are quite valid reasons for omitting this harsh word in this beautiful image of God's compassion and comfort. One can imagine a copyist writing that clause with some reluctance. This line, which serves as a transition to the even harsher words that follow in the next verses, offers us the opportunity to point out how the contrast between the Old Testament and the New Testament has been overplayed.

The Old Testament is often seen as a book whose God is fearful and in hot pursuit of evildoers. No one can escape the clutches of this justice-driven deity. But both this reading from Isaiah and many other readings from the Prophets and from Torah are full of the tender love of God. The God of the Hebrew Bible is a complex God and cannot be reduced to the easy absolutes of those who read the Bible selectively. This is true of the New Testament as well. Jesus has some harsh things to say of those who live without thought or care of anything or anyone but themselves. Neither testament should be reduced to a slogan, however.

The supposed contrast between the testaments further encourages us to stress the continuity between the two. There is a continuity between ancient Israel and Christianity, just as there is one between ancient Israel and modern Judaism and between ancient Israel and Islam. The three faiths all lay claim to the experience and traditions of ancient Israel and interpret them according to their own later experience and traditions.

God comforting in verse 13 is the recurrence of the idea that God does what others have been told to do. "Comfort" was the command in Isaiah 40:1. Now it is God who does the comforting.

The last image is that of the plant. "Like grass in spring" is the image for the flowering of one comforted and strengthened by God. Third Isaiah reverses the imagery of Isaiah 40:7: "The people are grass . . . the grass withers, the flower fades." But both Second and Third Isaiah agree that "the word of our God will endure for ever" (Isa. 40:8).

Retelling the Story

Joseph lay down on his mat and asked, "Mother, what is God like?"

Rebecca stopped her work and turned to her son. "What is God like?" she responded. "What makes you ask that? Perhaps you should talk to one of the men at the Temple."

Joseph turned his brown eyes to Rebecca, "I heard a man at the market today. He was calling out, 'Repent! Repent! Or God will strike you dead!' I was wondering what is God like, the one that we worship."

Rebecca sat down beside Joseph's mat and listened to the watchman sing out as he walked by. "Well, God is bigger than we can know. The Holy One of Israel is one to be loved and feared and honored. I do not know about the Torah and its teachings. But I know that we must always honor the Holy One in our actions, our thoughts, and our words."

"But what do you think God is like?" Joseph asked again. "Is he like the God that man was talking about? Will he kill us if we do not repent? Is God mean?"

"Oh, Joseph, I do not know. I'm only your mother, not a scholar or a priest." Rebecca was quiet, thinking about Joseph's question. "I guess when I think about God, may his name be blessed, I think about my mother and how gentle she was with her children."

"But why do you think about God like a mother? God must be strong like a king or a soldier!"

"Yes, God is strong like a king or a soldier. But to me, God is also loving and gentle and caring, like a mother. God gives us what we need to eat and drink. God gives us clothes

> Those who remember the destruction of the Temple and Jerusalem always leave a small portion of their house unplastered as a reminder. Or if they prepare a banquet, they will leave out some special dish so they will not forget. The women putting on their jewelry will leave one piece off, for only those who remember and mourn for Jerusalem will be able to rejoice its renewal. (*Sefer Ha-Aggadah* 198.21)

to wear and a shelter in which to live. God's provisions are abundant and generous.

"When I remember my mother nursing my little brother, I think that God must be like that—full of everything we need and giving it to us, his children, in the kindest, gentlest, most nurturing way that we can receive." Rebecca cradled her arms as if she were holding a baby. "Can you see that, Joseph? Can you see that kind of God?"

"It's like," Joseph said, "sometimes I still want to sit in your lap and have you hug me. I'm not a baby anymore, but I feel safe when you hold me. Do you think that God wants to keep us safe?"

"I think that the Holy One wishes every good thing for us, as a mother or father would wish for one of their children. I think that God treats us like a parent does, feeding us when we are hungry, carrying us when we are too tired to walk on our own. I think God delights in us. Remember when you were little and I would bounce you on my knee?"

Joseph smiled, "I would always laugh and want you to do it some more."

"And I would laugh, too," Rebecca answered. "I felt such joy in you. I think that God feels that joy about us."

Rebecca leaned over her son and kissed him on the forehead. "I think that God comforts us, just as a mother comforts her child." ·

"What do you mean, comfort, Mother?" Joseph asked.

"Do you remember when you were sick and I sat up with you all night? I washed your face with cool water and held you when you woke up crying. That was comforting. I was comforting you. When you hurt yourself and come to me, I comfort you by washing the wound and soothing your spirit. That is comfort.

We should remember the positive images that God has provided before the negative ones crowd them out. If we are having a bad time and want to say that God has sent hardship upon us flowing like a river, we can remember Isaiah's saying that God sends peace like a river instead. An ancient version of the power of positive thinking, no doubt. (*Sefer Ha-Aggadah* 792.27)

"That is what God does with us when we are hurting and fearful. God soothes us when we are sad and downcast. God holds us and rocks us and washes our wounds. God sits with us when we mourn and comforts us, as I have comforted you. That is what I think God is like, my son."

Joseph snuggled into his blankets and smiled, "I think I can feel the Holy One tucking me in."

Rebecca sat beside her son until he fell asleep. She asked the Holy One to watch over Joseph as he slept. Then she rose and went back to her tasks. As she worked, she praised God for God's tender love and care. *(Beth Richardson)*

The Call of Ezekiel

Ezekiel is possessed by a spirit and sent by God to speak to Israelites.

The Story

When I saw this I prostrated myself, and I heard a voice: 'Stand up, O man,' he said, 'and let me talk with you.' As he spoke, a spirit came into me and stood me on my feet, and I listened to him speaking. He said to me, 'O man, I am sending you to the Israelites, rebels who have rebelled against me. They and their forefathers have been in revolt against me to this very day, and this generation to which I am sending you is stubborn and obstinate. You are to say to them, "These are the words of the Lord GOD," and they will know that they have a prophet among them, whether they listen or whether in their rebelliousness they refuse to listen.'

Comments on the Story

This passage is part of the great opening scene of the book of Ezekiel. Ezekiel was a priest of the Solomonic Temple who was called to become a prophet. A man of Jerusalem, he was taken into exile and was forced to live in Mesopotamia. It is difficult to assess the man psychologically. He was a sensitive human being who accepted the mission of announcing God's judgment against Jerusalem and later the divine promises of restoration.

In this passage, the prophet is addressed with the intriguing expression *ben 'adam*. The traditional translation of the phrase is "son of man." The Hebrew simply identifies an individual as human. Probably the clearest English equivalent would be "a member of the human race." Modern versions have tried various ways to convey the idea. "Mortal" is the choice of the NRSV. The REB chooses the less inclusive "man." The prophet in the book of Ezekiel wants to emphasize the glory of God, and so he stresses the contrast between the human and the divine. The use of this term (appearing ninety-three times in Ezekiel) is one way to achieve this emphasis and to highlight the contrast.

The phrase as it appears in Ezekiel is not the origin of the expression Son of Man, used in the New Testament. In the Gospels, the reference is not to the book of Ezekiel but to the book of Daniel, specifically to Daniel 7:14. Ezekiel is never addressed by his personal name, differing in this from Jeremiah and Amos, who each has visions in which he is addressed by name. Ezekiel is the only prophet addressed as "son of man."

141

As a narrative development, this "call narrative" differs from Isaiah 6 or Jeremiah 1 because the prophet in this passage does not respond in words. In fact, he seems rather passive. He is told to get up (2:1 after having fallen on his face in 1:28), but it is a spirit that comes into Ezekiel that raises him up. Ezekiel does not speak until 4:14.

The reader finds many puzzles in the book of Ezekiel, and there is one that begins with the mention of "a spirit" in verse 2. The text is not clear on the source of this spirit, whether it is divine or human. The Hebrew word *ruah* means "wind" or "breath." The English word *spirit* is somewhat more specific than *ruah*. The book of Ezekiel does not exhibit a univocal usage and meaning of the term.

The passage emphasizes that Ezekiel is sent by God. This sending is the appointment of this individual to be the authorized spokesperson for the Lord. This appointment would have been important during the lifetime and activity of the prophet. But the call is also important for those who would pass on the words, those who would expand them, and those who, at a much later time, would read the words. Scholars do not agree on how many of the words of today's book Ezekiel is responsible for.

Ezekiel is sent to a particular people. Curiously the Hebrew reads "to the sons of Israel, to nations who rebel." The Greek version has "to the house of Israel who rebel." Differences in the texts always give scholars the opportunity to try to judge which version is the original. The Hebrew as we have it might contain revisions within it that had occurred after the Greek translation was made from it. And the Greek itself may have been revised after the translation. One cannot know which text is older.

In this particular case, each version has something characteristic of the whole book. The book does have oracles against the foreign nations, as the Hebrew of 2:3 might suggest. And Ezekiel generally speaks of the "house of Israel," as does the Greek of 2:3, rather than the "sons of Israel" of the Hebrew.

The depiction of the people, especially with regard to their past behavior, is striking: "nation[s] of rebels", "a people whose ancestors rebelled long ago." Ezekiel joins those prophets who look upon the history of Israel as one in which they were totally unfaithful. Some prophets thought of Israel as being faithful at one time and then falling away. Ezekiel sees no such history. Israel was a rebel from the start.

Perhaps one of the most haunting concerns of the book of Ezekiel is the theme of recognition. A persistent motivation given in Ezekiel is that God acts so that "they will know that I am Yahweh." Among the various reflections people have given for this motivation, probably two are more appealing. The first is simply that this divine statement of identity is found elsewhere in the ancient Near East. Ezekiel does not create this motivation on his own. The other is that human beings find their fulfillment in the recognition of who God is and in their sincere acknowledgment of the proper relation between God and humans.

The storyteller has various details on which to focus. The most obvious one is that of being "sent." Indeed, the idea of "sent ones" becomes prominent in all three later faiths—Judaism, Christianity, and Islam. In Christianity, an apostle is literally "one who is sent."

Retelling the Story

They will know that they have a prophet among them,
whether they listen or whether in their rebelliousness they refuse to listen.
(Ezek. 2:5)

Bertram McCawley was more used to standing before congregations than he was to facing the crowd who would question him today. These were the elected representatives of his home state, and, although he didn't think of it this way, they were just as unused to having a pastor testify in their chambers. The young Reverend McCawley tried to sit confidently without fidgeting in the chair that had been provided for him.

Finally, he was called forward, and a clerk held out a Bible to him and asked him to repeat an oath assuring his truthfulness. He had no religious opposition to swearing oaths but thought, even as he repeated the words, that such caution was unnecessary. It had been his unvarnished truthtelling that had gotten him invited to speak in the first place.

He had been called to the church he presently served a little over a year ago. He had become aware in the process of interviewing that a very prominent political family were members there. In the past year he had introduced a proposal at his denomination's yearly meeting to end official racial segregation in the congregations of that area. Much to his surprise, the proposal passed.

When he arrived back at his parsonage from that meeting, the messages from irate parishioners had already begun to accumulate on the table next to the phone. He came very close to being turned out that next week, but the older women of the church, among whom he had quite a following due to his skill at leading

> God approached the prophets through different senses. For example, Ezekiel experienced God both through seeing visions and breathing God's spirit in. Jeremiah was touched on the mouth and Habakkuk heard God. Even so, some prophets spoke in mysteries and also spoke in mysteries within mysteries. (*Sefer Ha-Aggadah* 476.73)

their Bible studies, had pleaded his youth and foolishness to their husbands and brothers. His supporters had prevailed in the voting, and he got off with a reminder that he was a religious leader and should stick to spiritual issues and avoid social and political ones.

I guess this isn't avoiding those issues, he thought to himself as he faced the legislative body that had invited him to be a representative of the religious community in the state. He wondered if they had any idea what they were in for. He certainly didn't.

"Reverend McCawley," began one questioner whose face he recognized from the newspaper, but whose name escaped him, "what is your view on the separation of the races?"

"I believe," he stopped to clear his throat, "that God created one race of people, the human race, and there is no particular reason why they should be separated from one another."

"Are you a native of this state?" another queried.

"I am, born and raised." He knew that what he had just said sounded even more like disloyalty to his roots, since he was one of them.

"Are you now or have you ever been a member of the Communist Party?" The questioner was red faced and jowled rather like a bulldog.

"No, sir, I'm just a Christian." He hoped for at least a sprinkling of laughter, but none was forthcoming.

"So you believe that there is no reason why our Christian women should not be allowed to associate with 'niggra' men?" the original speaker renewed his line of questions.

"I believe their wives already do associate with them, sir." He wondered if he had stepped over the line with his sarcasm.

"You know what I meant . . . our white women. Do you wish to be held in contempt?" the rage sounded a clear note in the legislator's voice.

"No, sir, I do not see the reason for the races to be divided in churches or schools or anywhere else. We are all children of God and as such none should be denied their rights."

"Including the right to vote in all-white primaries?"

"All-white primaries have been declared unconstitutional by the Supreme Court and will be held so when this state's case comes before them as well. There is coming a time, and it won't be long, when the white and negro citizens of this state will attend church and school together, ride the buses sitting wherever they

> The sages say that the title "ben 'adam" is an expression of love, friendship, and kinship. It can mean "son of righteous or worthy forebears," or "son of those who show compassion," or perhaps "son of those who humbled themselves before their Creator." (*Leviticus Rabbah* 2.7)

wish, go to the movies together, and even drink from the same water fountains. This is 1948, not 1848."

His antagonist paused and stared at the young preacher like he was a creature from another planet, "Do your church members know your views on this subject?"

"They do, and they will continue to hear them."

"Do you really expect to have a job when you get back home?" This time the laughter was deafening. *(Michael E. Williams)*

Long ago, it is told, the dogwood tree was one of the most majestic of all the trees in the forest. It had a tall, straight trunk with a large enough circumference that huge support beams could be hewn from it. The dogwood was very proud of both its looks and its usefulness. The other trees were sometimes envious of its strength and beauty.

One day woodcutters came and cut the dogwood and stripped it of its bark. Then the woodcutters harnessed their oxen so they could pull the dogwood to the hewing ground. There men with axes, hammers, and wedges hewed from it two square beams; then they cut the beams so that one was longer than the other. The two were notched to fit together and were taken to the military house.

Early one Friday morning workers came to get the notched beams of dogwood and placed them on a cart. Oxen pulling the cart moved slowly through the streets of the city to a place where prisoners awaiting execution were kept. The beams were unloaded from the cart and attached to form a cross.

After a time a man was led out of the prison. His back was still bleeding from the lashes he had received as part of his punishment. He wore the purple robe of royalty, and on his head was a crown made of branches from a thorn bush. A soldier ordered him to put his shoulder under the crosspiece and carry the cross to the place of execution. The cross was so heavy that it had to be dragged rather than carried, and the oxen who had brought the cross to the prison felt sorry for the new beast of burden who had to carry it by himself.

The last leg of the journey to the place of execution was the most difficult. On a hill, the cross was erected between two others after the man who had carried it was nailed to it at his hands and feet. If a tree could weep, the dogwood would have wept, and if it could have cried out it would have protested being used for such a cruel purpose.

The cross could hardly stand to listen to the groans of pain and feel the burden of the man nailed to it, pulling himself up by his nailed hands to take in a shallow breath before dropping his weight down again. Then the hoarse voice pleaded for those who had done the crucifying to be forgiven before he fell silent. Could God forgive such a heinous act? Could God transform one who had willingly played a part in this drama of death?

The dogwood asked God to change it so that its trunk could never again be used to make a cross. And the dogwood's request was granted. From that time to this, if you walk through the

> The rabbis say that God's intention to raise up the lowly tree and bring down the haughty one, and to dry up the green tree and make the dry tree flourish will be performed. God is not like humans in this respect; we often say we will do something and do not follow through. (*Genesis Rabbah* 53.1)

woods you will notice that the dogwood has a thin crooked trunk and small, almost delicate, branches. No one will ever be able to use the dogwood for a cross again.

You may also notice that when the dogwood blooms its cross-shaped blossoms, whether white or pink, have brown "nail holes" on the end of each petal and a "crown" in the center. These are reminders of the suffering of the one who hung on the cross. When we see the blossoms, we are to tell this story to our children and grandchildren. *(Michael E. Williams)*

Sour Grapes No More

Ezekiel would rather not blame society for the sins of an individual.

The Story

This word of the LORD came to me: 'What do you all mean by repeating this proverb in the land of Israel:
Parents eat sour grapes,
and their children's teeth are set on edge? 'As I live, says the Lord GOD, this proverb will never again be used by you in Israel. Every living soul belongs to me; parent and child alike are mine. It is the person who sins that will die.

'You say that the Lord acts without principle? Listen, you Israelites! It is not I who act without principle; it is you. If a righteous man turns from his righteousness, takes to evil ways, and dies, it is because of these evil ways that he dies. Again, if a wicked man gives up his wicked ways and does what is just and right, he preserves his life; he has seen his offences and turned his back on them all, and so he will not die; he will live. "The Lord acts without principle," say the Israelites. No, it is you, Israel, that acts without principle, not I.

'Therefore I shall judge every one of you Israelites on his record, says the Lord GOD. Repent, renounce all your offences, or your iniquity will be your downfall. Throw off the load of your past misdeeds; get yourselves a new heart and a new spirit. Why should you Israelites die? I have no desire for the death of anyone. This is the word of the Lord GOD.'

Comments on the Story

This reading is a combination of the beginning and the conclusion of Ezekiel 18, which is the true unit. The fairly long passage has two major sections: Verses 1-20 discusses a proverb about responsibility and hence punishment for sins passing from one generation to another, and verses 21-32 treats the issue of whether God's justice is really just, whether God really pays attention to repentance.

The discussion on generational responsibility begins with a proverb that the prophet quotes and then argues against. Actually, the idea that later generations suffer because of the sins of previous ones recurs in various parts of the Bible. Exodus 20:5 is probably the clearest example: "I, the LORD your God, am a jealous God, punishing the children for the sins of the parents to the third and fourth generation of those who reject me."

Ezekiel sets out to correct that idea. He is not alone in that effort. Deuteronomy 24:16 directly states: "Parents are not to be put to death for their children, nor children for their parents; each one may be put to death only for his own sin." No doubt, the situation that would have led most directly to the debate among the people over a presumably popular saying was the fall of Jerusalem (587 B.C.E.) or the first deportation (598 B.C.E.) and the events that led up to the fall and second deportation.

The book of Jeremiah also records this proverb. In Jeremiah 31:29-30 there is not much argumentation against the saying. The text simply claims that the saying will no longer be repeated. The Hebrew word for "proverb," *mashal,* is the same word used of the proverbs collected in the book of that name attributed to Solomon. As Lord John Russell cleverly said, "A proverb is one person's wit and everybody's wisdom." Actually, we don't know how many people really did apply this proverb to the political situation of the Southern Kingdom in the sixth century B.C.E.

We do know that wreaking punishment on the family of a criminal seems to have been a standard practice in the ancient Near East. There remains a Hittite reflection: "If anyone arouses the anger of a god, does the god take revenge on him alone? Does he not take revenge on his wife, his children, his descendants, his kin, his slaves, and slave-girls, his cattle and sheep together with his crop, and will utterly destroy him?" The books of Ezekiel and Jeremiah change this conviction for Israel and their depiction of their God.

The theme of the prophet's efficacy in the face of the people's repentance also raises questions. During the period immediately before the exile, the prophets generally understood their task to be that of calling the people to repentance. The prophets of the eighth century had appeared mainly as messengers of doom. Israel had sinned and now must bear the punishment of its sin.

Prophets come now who, under the influence of the Deuteronomic teaching (or does this idea come from the editors of their books?) who preach a "turning" to God, a repentance. Both "turn" and "repent" are expressed by the same Hebrew word. The conviction that God is moved by repentance can be seen in the opening chapters of the book of Judges (a book that was edited shortly before the fall of Jerusalem).

Thus Ezekiel argues that God's ways are not without principle or without logic. God has determined that good actions will lead to good results. Ezekiel assures his readers of this principle so that they will be motivated to live in the ways that God has established for Israel to live.

Indeed, God wants people to behave in a way that leads to life. All persons bear the responsibility for their own lives. An individual can so live as to save that life or lose it. The prophet here is clear that God does not want death, only life.

There are some curious things in this passage. Everyone knows that good people do not always prosper (or sometimes even survive). The friends who come to discuss with Job his fate arc convinced of the truth of the idea that the good always prosper. But Job is not of that opinion, nor does he ever become convinced of it. Qohelet simply denies it. Ezekiel's position on this point is clearly not universally applicable.

Another very distinctive point in this reading at verse 31 is that the readers are told, "Get [the Hebrew reads ' make'] yourselves a new heart and a new spirit." This statement surprises one who has read both elsewhere in Ezekiel and also in Jeremiah that a new heart and a new spirit are obtained only through the action of God.

There is a final point on the translation: In verse 29, the REB reads as if Israel were addressed directly and personally. This is a looser translation than some would prefer. Only once in the book of Ezekiel is Israel spoken to in direct singular address (vocative), and that is at 13:4. The Hebrew of Ezekiel 18:29 reads, "O house of Israel."

Retelling the Story

> Every living soul belongs to me; parent and child alike are mine. It is the person who sins that will die.
>
> (Ezek. 18:4)

Angela looked down at the tiny form that lay in the infant bed. Tubes entered its nose and mouth; monitors were attached to its chest and finger. An IV offered the child both nourishment and medicine that should have come from its mother's breast. Technically, nursing school had prepared her for her tasks in neonatal intensive care. Emotionally, nothing could have prepared her.

When she had first begun work at City Memorial she thought it would be relatively easy to keep an appropriate emotional distance from her patients. After all, they were newborns with no developed personality to speak of. They couldn't tell you stories about their families, fond memories or hopes for the future. Many of them were too weak or too heavily sedated to cry. She would simply practice the best medicine she had learned, do all that she could, cut her losses when it wasn't enough, and leave the work at the hospital when she went home.

Angela could not have been more mistaken. Their little faces, so similar in their reddish hue and wrinkles, would float up in her dreams and break her heart with their unvoiced cries. During her worst nights they were all her children; she knew that in the certainty that only dreams can offer. Despite having never given birth herself, she had come to know a mother's distress and troubled sleep. She had hundreds of babies all crying for her to do something to

Once there was a fox who wanted to get the better of a wolf, so the fox told the wolf to go into the courtyard of a home just as they were preparing the Sabbath meal. The fox told the wolf that he would be welcomed and invited to share the meal with the family. But when the wolf entered the courtyard, the people there beat him with sticks within an inch of his life, and he barely escaped.

The wolf went looking for the fox to get revenge for the trick that the fox played on him. When the wolf found that trickster, however, the fox said, "They only beat you because your father had helped them prepare the meal once, then ate every bit of it before anyone else had a chance to take a bite."

"Why should they beat me because of something my father did?" asked the wolf.

"Because they believe that the fox eats sour grapes and the children's teeth are set on edge, but let me show you a place where you can eat your fill without being beaten." The fox proceeded to lead the wolf to a well and pointed to the reflection of the moon. "See. There is a big round cheese for you. Just let yourself down in the bucket and you will find bread and other food there for you to eat."

So the wolf got in the bucket only to find himself flying down the well shaft until he hit the water. The wolf called up to the fox, "Help me. What am I to do now?"

"The Lord will deliver the righteous," replied the fox as he went on his merry way. (*Sefer Ha-Aggadah* 245.194)

ease their agony. The nightmarish aspect of the dream was that she knew that there was nothing she could do.

Recently, Angela had begun to attend worship services at a church near her apartment, something she had given up as soon as her parents gave in to her adolescent will and allowed her to remain in bed on Sunday mornings. She had returned to church out of a need to gain some perspective on her life, to understand some of the suffering that surrounded her daily. She liked the people in the congregation, and the pastor was friendly and interesting to listen to, but she had not discovered what she was looking for.

Just yesterday the pastor had preached on a scripture lesson from Ezekiel that had angered and confused her. The prophet seemed to be saying that everyone got just what he or she deserved. The preacher pointed out that Ezekiel threw out the old idea that people were punished for their parents' sin. But, she had wanted to say, what about those who are born addicted to cocaine or are HIV positive through no fault of their own? If that wasn't a case of the parents' eating sour grapes and the children's teeth being set on edge, she didn't know what was. How could the prophet and the preacher be so glib about such an obvious case of undeserved punishment?

Grown-ups cause a lot of their own problems, she was willing to give them that. But what about the babies whom she cared for—those born with most of their internal organs on the outside rather than the inside, those whose brains were denied oxygen for an extended time so that they would never become the people they were meant to be? Not only was it blatantly unjust, but also it didn't make sense. The prophet and the preacher seemed to have such simple answers about who suffered and why, but they didn't apply in her world.

As she checked the vital signs on the infant who lay before her, "Baby Girl Doe," she was calm and professional to anyone looking on, but if they could have gotten a glimpse of her soul they would have heard her screaming out to God the unfairness of it all. She would defy anyone to accuse these babies of deserving what they suffered. Whether inflicted upon them by parental sins or fate she could not say. But she would not claim that some just God was punishing them for some imagined sins, as the prophet and pastor had so easily concluded. Such a God would be a monster. Whatever God was to her or would be in the future she wasn't sure. She would keep her silent vigil at the bedside of her tiny patients and comfort them as she could, if only in her dreams. It was all she could think to do. *(Michael E. Williams)*

> The idea that each sinner would suffer for that individual's sins was softened a bit by the sages. When asked what God meant by this warning, they replied that when God was asked what it meant, he said the sinner should repent so that the sins would be forgiven. The sages understood these words as an enticement to repentance, not a counsel of despair. (*Sefer Ha-Aggadah* 556.195)

The Watchman

The watchman who does not warn sinners is responsible for their death.

The Story

I have appointed you, O man, a watchman for the Israelites, and you must pass to them any warnings you receive from me. If I pronounce sentence of death on a person because he is wicked and you do not speak out to dissuade him from his ways, that person will die because of his sin, but I shall hold you answerable for his death. However, if you have warned him to give up his ways, and he persists in them, he will die because of his sin, but you will have saved yourself.

'O man, say to the Israelites: You complain, "We are burdened by our sins and offences; we are pining away because of them, and despair of life." Tell them: As I live, says the Lord GOD, I have no desire for the death of the wicked. I would rather that the wicked should mend their ways and live. Give them up, give up your evil ways. Israelites, why should you die?'

Comments on the Story

This reading brings together many themes or elements of the book of Ezekiel. Ezekiel, in exile, is concerned first with showing that the holiness of God requires that the Jerusalem Temple be destroyed because of the impurity he sees in it. But his book also predicts the restoration of that city in a new existence.

This particular passage is strategically located immediately before the brief narrative in which the prophet hears the news of the fall of Jerusalem and regains his ability to speak. This may be a time when his words of accusation and doom are replaced by words of warmth and hope.

The prophet is addressed again in the form specific to Ezekiel: "son of man," here rendered "O man." The persistent usage of this title in the book of Ezekiel impresses on the reader the contrast between what is human and what is divine, the holy and mysterious who is present only through "glory."

God's address to the prophet begins with the reminder that it was God who called Ezekiel to the role of prophet. In 33:2, there is an example of a country whose people determine that they need a sentinel or watchman and who then select one. But this passage, addressed directly to the prophet, asserts that he is not selected by the people but appointed by God. He is to speak on behalf of God to the people, warning them of the punishment that might come.

Until this point in Israel's history, prophecy could be a matter of life and death. With the classical eighth-century prophets Amos, Hosea, and Micah, the message seemed to be exclusively one of doom. With Isaiah and others, the words seemed to contain promises and hope, and Jeremiah is depicted as a prophet who calls to repentance. Second Isaiah will try to be the most consoling of all the prophets.

The role of the prophet seems to have demanded increasingly more out of those called to be a prophet. Little is told of the demands put on Hosea and Amos by their prophetic ministry. Isaiah seems to have had only certain periods of prophetic activity. Jeremiah felt himself threatened by those Jerusalemites who planned to take his life. But Ezekiel in this passage is told by God that his life is at stake in this prophetic task. If the prophet is remiss in warning the wicked, the prophet will have to answer for the death of the sinners.

The Israelites (or "house of Israel," as Ezekiel calls his audience in exile) appear here to be worried about the sin that they are conscious of. They feel weighed down and weakened by the thought and guilt of their deeds. Of course, it is not stated how the prophet knew the thoughts of his audience; one might guess that Ezekiel is putting thoughts into their heads. At any rate, he wonders what the future holds. He thinks anyone must wonder where there can be life after what must have seemed the greatest catastrophe, the collapse of the city of God.

On this point and at this place, Ezekiel is clear. God does not delight in death. God chooses life for the people. God wants all human beings to live. This thought is an echo, perhaps, of a verse in Deuteronomy: "I summon heaven and earth to witness against you this day: I offer you the choice of life or death, blessing or curse. Choose life and you and your descendants will live" (Deut. 30:19).

It is not surprising that the prophet pleads with his audience. "Give them up, give up your evil ways." Ezekiel is convinced of the efficacy of repentance. Therein lies hope for the Israelites. The character of God is such that repentance bends the heart and mind of God.

Ezekiel is not specific about the evil ways of his audience. He simply says that whatever they are, repentance can change everything. (In Ezekiel 8:12, the prophet sees what his audience has in their "shrines of their carved images"— he means their minds— namely, "abominations.")

This passage provides today's reader with a consoling example of Ezekiel's speeches to the exiles. Ezekiel both realizes that the people's sins have brought on them this disaster and is convinced that God wants them to be fully alive.

Probably the storyteller would want to focus on the message of hope for life. The prophet is one who addresses a people that is troubled and in doubt of the future. Or the teller might emphasize the culpability of all who remain silent in the face of great sin.

Retelling the Story

> However, if you have warned [a sinner] to give up [sinful] ways, and he persists in them, [the sinner] will die because of his sin, but you will have saved yourself.
>
> (Ezek. 33:9)

The service had ended, and the visiting preacher was greeting those who had attended the last night of camp meeting. Some had been there all four nights, and Stephen had been impressed. He had chosen for his sermon during this concluding service a story about someone who had been a "window into God" for him. He had hoped that his remembrances would spark recollections for those who were listening as well. Some of those who had attended were confirming that he had been successful, at least partially, as they told him of those persons who had held a similar sacred place in their lives.

An older woman who the night before had told him of her mistreatment at the hands of a group of good religious folk in the area was standing quietly at the periphery of the animated conversation of well wishes and good-byes. Near her was a young man hanging back from the crowd too.

After the crowd had dispersed, the young man approached and handed Stephen a small pamphlet, saying, "If you died tonight and found yourself face to face with God, what would you say to him that would allow him to let you into heaven?"

Great, thought Stephen, *all I need is some religious nut trying to save me.* He had experienced this before but never just after he had preached. His subconscious mind must have been working, because he was almost as surprised as his questioner when he heard the words, "Your grace!" come out of his mouth.

"What does that mean?" the intense young man wanted to know.

"It means that nothing I have done qualifies me to even stand in God's presence. I depend entirely for God's grace for that." Stephen was rather pleased that he had been able to answer without exhibiting any of the anger that was beginning to rise into his throat.

The young man stammered a bit, "B-b-but God is a judge too." Then he began to quote something from Revelation about the devil and all his angels and a lake of fire.

"Yes, God is my judge, but you are not!" Stephen emphasized the word *you,* hoping to put an end to the conversation.

"I haven't been a Christian very long. . . . " The young questioner rambled on about the plan of salvation and all the people who were misled, although they were members of various churches. Somewhere in the middle of his obviously memorized spiel Stephen tuned the man out. He realized that his challenger had listened to his sermon and decided on that basis that the preacher

159

When God's people sin it is God who seeks out an advocate for them. Remember that God went to Abraham to talk over a response to the sins of Sodom. The sages say that God went for the express purpose of allowing Abraham to defend the people against divine wrath. It is not God's wish that anyone should die but that all should turn back to God and live. (*Sefer Ha-Aggadah* 557.207)

was not going to make the final cut on judgment day. Perhaps he wouldn't even make the first cut.

Anger made Stephen's voice tremble ever so slightly as he began, "And you don't think I'm a Christian." Stephen reached toward the startled young man with the hand that held the pamphlet he had hardly glanced at. "Here, take your tract back. This conversation is over."

The young man took the pamphlet as he drew back, still looking directly at the preacher, "I just wanted to tell you . . . at least your soul won't be on my hands . . . " Then he turned abruptly and disappeared into the night.

It took a while for Stephen to realize that he was still shaking from the encounter. He turned to see the older woman with whom he had talked the night before easing toward him. She came close to him, closer than was normally comfortable, and said in a voice that was almost a whisper, "I understood what you were talking about."

Then she too was gone. *(Michael E. Williams)*

The Shepherd God

The good shepherd protects the lean sheep from fat sheep who feed themselves too much.

The Story

For the Lord GOD says: Now I myself shall take thought for my sheep and search for them. As a shepherd goes in search of his sheep when his flock is scattered from him in every direction, so I shall go in search of my sheep and rescue them, no matter where they were scattered in a day of cloud and darkness. I shall lead them out from the nations, gather them in from different lands, and bring them home to their own country. I shall shepherd them on the mountains of Israel and by her streams, wherever there is a settlement. I shall feed them on good grazing-ground, and their pasture will be Israel's high mountains. There they will rest in good pasture, and find rich grazing on the mountains of Israel. I myself shall tend my flock, and find them a place to rest, says the Lord GOD. I shall search for the lost, recover the straggler, bandage the injured, strengthen the sick, leave the healthy and strong to play, and give my flock their proper food.

'Therefore, the Lord GOD says to them: Now I myself shall judge between the fat sheep and the lean. You push aside the weak with flank and shoulder, you butt them with your horns until you have scattered them in every direction. Therefore I shall save my flock, and they will be ravaged no more; I shall judge between one sheep and another.

'I shall set over them one shepherd to take care of them, my servant David; he will care for them and be their shepherd. I, the LORD, shall be their God, and my servant David will be prince among them. I, the LORD, have spoken.'

Comments on the Story

The image of sheep, with which this passage opens, follows immediately from the preceding section. There the prophet is attacking the false leaders of the people. He accuses them of being selfish and of not serving and caring for the people. In the view expressed there, those leaders are in positions of leadership only for their own benefit and to the detriment of the people.

The image of shepherds for the king was common throughout the ancient Near East. Texts in languages such as Sumerian, Hittite, and Akkadian all record this image. And Israel takes over the image easily from the neighboring cultures presumably at a fairly early stage in Israel's history.

161

In this passage, God says that the role of leadership has been abused by the leaders. The leaders do not feed the flock; instead, they feed themselves on the flock. Now God will step in and lead the people. The details of this leadership, or the means by which it will be executed, are not even hinted at. God simply says that new leadership is needed. God will step in personally to lead the people.

Ezekiel does not seem to allow that God had already been leading Israel. Other parts of the Hebrew Bible do suggest that, for example Psalm 80:1. But this new leadership is special. God will bring the exiles home from whatever lands they had been exiled to. The idea of bringing exiles back to their homeland is not uncommon in ancient writings. But for Israel it would mean the end of the exile and the rebuilding of Jerusalem.

God even says that the lost will be sought out. No one will escape this being found. (Christians may think of the New Testament and the parable of the good Shepherd; this passage in Ezekiel may well be a source of the ideas in the parable.) The nations will no longer detain or hold captive the people of God.

The text suggests a time somewhat later than the dates of Ezekiel in the sixth century. The exile to Babylon was but one of the various departures from the land. Migrations occurred in other directions—to Egypt, to Asia Minor, and eventually to Rome. Thus the return would occur later, when the people of Israel were scattered throughout many nations.

Ezekiel speaks with love and affection of the land from which he was exiled. He (or a later writer) enjoys imagining the mountains and streams, the fields and pastures. The richness of the description betrays attachment that goes beyond the ordinary.

Unfortunately, the REB throws a feminine reference into this scene. (The RSV and the Hebrew have no possessive pronouns here.) The Bible consistently refers to Israel as "he" and never as "she." The REB elsewhere confuses the gender of Israel. In Jeremiah 2:1 Israel becomes "her" while at Jeremiah 2:14 Israel is "he." The Hebrew has masculine singular in both verses.

But even within this vision of a time when all will be fulfilled, our text poses a separation between the good and the bad, "the straggler, the injured, and the sick" over against "the healthy and the strong." This tension in the text may suggest that it was written at a time when there was a sharp division within the postexilic community between the returning establishment and those who had stayed.

The text grows stronger at verse 21: "You push aside the weak . . . you butt them . . . until you have scattered them in every direction." The strength of the oppressors within the community is quite deep. The text seems to record the bitter feelings of a group that has been treated with contempt and injustice. They have little hope unless God intervenes.

And God gives that promise: "I shall save . . . I shall judge." Then God steps aside, as it were, and announces one who will take the divine place: "My servant David" will shepherd the flock. The promise of a restored monarchy is dramatic in the postexilic community. The book of Ezekiel contains vibrant expression of this hope.

Most likely, this passage refers to more than restoration of the previous political setup. The hope expressed is for the ultimate time of fulfillment, the messianic times. The Bible depicts this time of fulfillment, coming about in various ways. Quite frequently there is a human being whom God uses to usher in the time, an anointed one, the Messiah. At other times, God acts without an intermediary. In this passage, the emphasis falls on both the messianic figure and on the action of God bringing the fulfillment.

The storyteller might focus on the conditions in which the promise is given or on the promise of fulfillment and on its details. It is not hard to imagine fat sheep and lean sheep in many of our subcultures, such as business, religion, and politics.

Retelling the Story

'I shall set over them one shepherd to take care of them, my servant David; he will care for them and be their shepherd.'

(Ezek. 34:23)

Samuel was just learning the rigorous tasks of shepherding. He still waited with adults or older boys through the long nights and difficult days. He had yet to be left alone overnight with the flocks and herds. He was a bit irked with his father for not trusting him enough to allow him to shepherd alone. He imagined that David had taken full care of Jesse's sheep by the time he was Samuel's age.

On the other hand, it was comforting when an emergency arose to know that someone more experienced would be there to handle it. Young King David had spoken of fighting off lions and bears before he faced the Philistine giant. Samuel had no desire to face a wild beast alone. The night with its array of mysterious sounds made him nervous enough.

Tonight he would be among those who would remain awake through the first watch to protect the sheep. He didn't mind the first watch so very much, since he found it easier to stay awake when he had sleep to look for-

> One sage said that this passage offered a most important metaphor for the place the righteous would have in the world to come. They will be like sheep in the mountains pastured on good grazing land. God alone will be their shepherd and they will live in contentment. (*Genesis Rabbah* 33.1)

ward to rather than being awakened from a sound sleep, only to have to force himself to stay alert. Besides, the conversation among the shepherds would be pretty lively for the first few hours of the night. This made the night sounds a little less frightening.

The sheep had quieted down earlier and would be settled for the night. The older shepherds had already begun to tell their jokes, some of which he wondered if he was really old enough to hear. He was glad for the darkness, for sometimes his cheeks burned with embarrassment, which he was sure would be evident to the others in daylight. He never joined in the conversation except to laugh at the appropriate times, even if he had no idea why a particular punch line was supposed to be funny.

Shepherds were not particularly well thought of in the towns like nearby Bethlehem. Perhaps the wrong people had heard some of the jokes the shepherds told at night. Samuel didn't know the reason why—except that his father said that it was as honest a trade as being a priest or a king, so long as each of those callings was practiced with honesty. Besides, Samuel's father told him, the shepherds were appreciated when the sheep returned whole and healthy to someone's sheepfold, or when those who served at the Temple needed a sacrifice.

Samuel had stopped listening to the others and was in another place, a place deep inside himself, when he heard a fluttering sound. He thought to himself that this was not the season for birds to migrate in flocks. Then there came a sound that reminded him distinctly of singing, except more beautiful than any singing he had ever heard. He could barely make out the words. "Peace on earth and goodwill. . . . Peace on earth and goodwill. . . . Do not be afraid. . . . Do not be afraid."

And he was not afraid. *(Michael E. Williams)*

> Since the Torah was given from a mountain, then the compassion of those who follow its way must be strong and expansive as the mountains, say the ancient rabbis. (*Leviticus Rabbah* 27.1)

A Fleshy Heart

A hardened, stone heart will be replaced with a fleshy human heart, which is obedient to God's law.

The Story

I shall take you from among the nations, and gather you from every land, and bring you to your homeland. I shall sprinkle pure water over you, and you will be purified from everything that defiles you; I shall purify you from the taint of all your idols. I shall give you a new heart and put a new spirit within you; I shall remove the heart of stone from your body and give you a heart of flesh. I shall put my spirit within you and make you conform to my statutes; you will observe my laws faithfully. Then you will live in the land I gave to your forefathers; you will be my people, and I shall be your God.'

Comments on the Story

This passage comes after a section that addresses the mountains of Israel (36:1-15). Earlier, in chapter 6, the mountains of Israel were addressed and cursed. In this section, they are readdressed and now receive blessing and promise of fruitfulness; the promise continues in this passage.

Now the divine will is that God gather the Israelites "from among the nations and from every land" (v. 24). One may be inclined to wonder when this text was written and what the writer was thinking. It seems to assume that there are exiles in many places. People were deported, in fact, only to Mesopotamia after the fall of both the Northern and the Southern kingdoms. So "the nations" and "all the lands" appear as an exaggeration if one is thinking about exiles. Many people may have left the land of Israel for economic reasons at any time.

For the goal of the return, the REB translates "to your homeland," and that phrase fits the setting well. But there may be an additional allusion. The word rendered "homeland" is *'adamah,* the same word used in Genesis 2 for the dust that God uses to form Adam, the "Earthling." Ezekiel seems to refer to Genesis 2 more clearly in the next reading.

God is depicted in preceding verses as judging Israel to be impure, a condition that rendered their homeland (same word, even though REB here has "soil") impure (v. 17). God will sprinkle pure water on the people, and thus they will be purified. This action represents the thinking of a priest, Ezekiel's original calling. The priest is concerned with the ritual impurities that the tradition carefully enumerated.

The text becomes even more specific about impurity. The people are told that they will be purified "from the taint of all your idols" (v. 25). The book of Ezekiel is quite surprising when it accuses the readers of idol worship. There is little evidence that the exiles had idols. Thus the text may employ a symbolic use of the word.

A more encouraging idea is the gift of a new heart and a new spirit. Biblically, the heart is the source of thought, and the spirit is that which gives life. Thus one who receives this double gift will be totally renewed.

God is the giver of this gift, the only one who can give it. This view differs from Ezekiel 18, in which readers are told that they themselves should get new hearts and new spirits. The present passage seems to fit more with other thinkers of this time, especially Jeremiah, who seem to think that humanity is clearly incapable of a true response to God. God alone is able help a person serve God and remain true to what God demands.

The promise is that God will remove the heart of stone and replace it with a heart of flesh. It is a pleasure to see that the text obviously sees flesh in itself as good, not something to be feared or to be suspicious of. God gives a heart of flesh, a truly human heart, by which one can be pleasing to other humans and to God.

With the new flesh comes the spirit of God. This expression, of course, does not have the Christian doctrinal idea of the third divine person of the Trinity. The spirit of God is the means by which God effects the world and affects human beings. This expression is another way of saying that in the time of fulfillment, people will not be left simply to themselves. God will empower them to do what they should do.

The task that Ezekiel sees for the purified people is to observe all that God has already laid out for them. Faithful obedience to the statutes and the laws is something anticipated for the age of fulfillment. This adherence to the regulations is found in other writings of this period. Jeremiah 31:31-34 speaks of that time in the imagery of a new covenant: God will put the law "within them, writing it on their hearts." The book of Jeremiah sees law as part of the time of fulfillment.

"Then live in the land I gave your forefathers." The Bible presents a variety of views on the land. In some parts of the Pentateuch, the land and its inhabitants are a real threat to Israel and to its continued survival. The land is so closely connected to its earlier inhabitants, the Canaanites, that Israel needs to be vigilant constantly to preserve itself from the seductions of the land and the people. In other places, the land is portrayed as fruitful, teeming in all the delights that befit the people of God. God promised this land to Israel's ancestors; Israel must maintain the land free of impurity, lest the nation lose the land God has given.

Finally, the passage closes with that mutual relationship of Yahweh as the God of Israel and Israel as the people of Yahweh. This is the famous covenant formula, which defines the members in this agreement. It is somewhat surprising that Ezekiel does not mention or discuss at any length the covenant at Sinai, between God and Israel. Perhaps Ezekiel was not enthusiastic about using the metaphor of covenant, for it had probably come into prevalence only recently. Whether these words are from Ezekiel or not, the book connects him with the dominant covenant theology of its time.

Retelling the Story

'I shall remove the heart of stone from your body and give you a heart of flesh.'

(Ezek. 36:26*b*)

A Litany of Renewal

We have heard the cry of children and have turned away, saying, "They are not ours. What do they have to do with us?"
Take away our hearts of stone and give us hearts of flesh, O God who cares for all children.

We have heard the sobs of mothers whose soldier sons will never return to embrace them again and have turned away, saying, "He was our enemy."
Take away our hearts of stone and give us hearts of flesh, O God of both our friends and our enemies.

Some sages contend that it was never the priests that made people clean. It was and is God alone who can cleanse us of any uncleanliness. (*Sefer Ha-Aggadah* 497.98)

We have heard the angry voices of those who have been denied what we take for granted, and we have turned away, saying, "You know how those people are. What reason could they possibly have to be so angry?"
Take away our hearts of stone and give us hearts of flesh, O God who was born in flesh among the poor.

We have heard the groans of the sick and dying and turned away, saying, "They brought it upon themselves. If they had only . . . "
Take away our hearts of stone and give us hearts of flesh, O God, who never blamed the ill for their illnesses but cured or comforted them.

We have seen the aged tied to their beds or wheelchairs and turned away, saying, "What a shame that they are such a hardship on us."
Take away our hearts of stone and give us hearts of flesh, O God, who sought honor for our mothers and fathers.

The Torah is called a stone since it was on tablets of stone that the decalogue was recorded. But the impulse to do evil is also called a stone since God promised to take away our hearts of stone; in other words our hearts intent on doing other than God wishes us to do. (*Leviticus Rabbah* 35.5)

We have turned away and turned away until there is no place to turn but to you, but as soon as we do we hear their cries and sobs. We hear their angry voices and their groans. We see all their faces, and they are your face, O God who called us to love as you love.
Take away our hearts of stone, O God.
Take away our hearts of stone, O God.
Take away our hearts of stone, O God.
And give us hearts like yours. Amen.

(Michael E. Williams)

Dry Bones

Ezekiel's prophecy restores life to the valley of dry bones.

The Story

The LORD's hand was upon me, and he carried me out by his spirit and set me down in a plain that was full of bones. He made me pass among them in every direction. Countless in number and very dry, they covered the plain. He said to me, 'O man, can these bones live?' I answered, 'Only you, Lord GOD, know that.' He said, 'Prophesy over these bones; say: Dry bones, hear the word of the LORD.'

Comments on the Story

This reading is probably the most famous passage in the book of Ezekiel. Its influence has gone far beyond the Bible, into the world of music and art. From it comes African American spiritual, which celebrates the marvelous connecting of bones into human bodies and their hearing the Word of the Lord. And it inspired the mosaics of the synagogue of Dura-Europos in Syria, now reproduced in the Yale Museum, in which the dead bodies return to life and the tombs become empty of their previous holdings.

The opening of the passage is dramatic and impressive. The formula "the Lord's hand was on me" is surely awe-provoking in itself. The image of the Lord's hand also suggests to some commentators an ecstatic trance. The phrase was used only four times (1:3; 3:14, 22; 33:22) before in Ezekiel. The vision given here is important enough to connect with the extraordinary experiences that precede it in the book. Some commentators see the episode as a real experience; others see it more as a literary composition.

The prophet is taken to "a plain" (as in 3:22), and he is set down in the midst of numerous bones, human bones that have been drying as they lie out in the blazing sun of the Middle East. Not only is the prophet to behold them and see their dryness and hopelessness but also he is told to pass through them to gain firsthand conviction of their futile state. The reader feels the eerie quality of that walk through the debris of human failure.

The scene is unique in the Bible and produces strange effects on different readers. Ezekiel surely is the prophet whose book contains the most surprising and sometimes unpleasant effects on the reader.

The prophet is addressed in the usual way but with a question that no one would want to be asked in this setting: "O man, can these bones live?" In the context, this translation is suitable. The question actually could be rendered as easily, "Will these bones live?" The answer is obvious, but Ezekiel knows that he should not say no. He simply answers that God knows the answer.

Then the odd command, "Prophesy to them!" Speak to dead, dry bones? What could be more inane?

But the prophet obeys, and the miracle begins. The drama of the situation is overpowering. The bones come together and begin to resume the position of living bones, to take on sinews, and finally to get flesh back on them. The miracle is done: They are bodies again.

But then comes the culminating event. The bones had become the impossible—human bodies with all their parts. But this was not enough to symbolize what the intention was. God says they need breath to make them alive. The prophet is commanded to finish the task by bringing breath into them. The winds bring the breath that makes them fully alive.

The text plays on the Hebrew word *ruah* delightfully. *Ruah* is rendered in English as "wind," "breath," "spirit." So Ezekiel is carried by the *ruah* of God (v. 1), prophesies to the four *ruahs* (Hebrew *ruhot*; v. 9), and *ruah* comes into the bodies to make them alive (v. 10). The divine and the human can seem to intermingle. The miracle is complete through the word of the prophet.

Many commentators have seen a connection between this passage and Genesis 2. There God makes a body out of clay. It is a little mannequin, a body without life or breath. God breathes on it, into it, and only then does it get the breath that is life.

If one wonders where Ezekiel might have gotten the idea for the imagery of the field, the possible source appears when he calls the bodies "these slain." The inspiration for the passage, the idea that God used to get the writer going, is the reality of war. Only after warfare might one find a field of bodies, so many that one could walk among them for some time without coming to an end.

A surprise comes in the words "I shall open your graves and bring you up from them" (v. 12). One does not expect the appearance of graves; the author likes the idea and repeats it in verse 13. The notion of opening graves is even more dramatic than simply coming upon a field of dry bones. Perhaps the author (or better an editor or copyist) got carried away with the idea of revivification. Probably the author was not thinking of an individual's life after death in a resurrected body.

This emphasis on regular, communal life as we know it is brought home by the divine words, "I shall . . . restore you to the land of Israel." It is the future life of the returned exiles that the text envisions.

The vision of the valley of dry bones ends with a favorite idea of Ezekiel, that people will know who Yahweh is. "You [my people] will know that I am the LORD." God wants recognition—especially the recognition that Israel itself will give God.

Retelling the Story

"[God] said to me, 'O man, can these bones live?' " (Ezek. 37:3*a*)

Zeke Dreadful Water was on a pilgrimage. His journey had begun in Southwestern North Carolina not far from Chattanooga, Tennessee, and would take him all the way to his birthplace outside Tahlequah, Oklahoma. He had grown up in the "Indian Territory," a member of the Eastern Band of the Cherokee. His ancestors had lived in North Georgia before it had been given that name by European settlers. They had hunted the hills and "hollers" of Middle Tennessee, through which he was passing presently. Later that same landscape would see his people die across each of its many miles as they were removed to the west.

The reference to the bones being dry, according to the rabbis, is to say that they have no marrow in them. And the marrow that would give them life is good deeds. (*Sefer Ha-Aggadah* 456.509)

The school of Shammai and the school of Hillel disagreed about the significance of this passage for the world to come. The School of Shammai said that in this world the skin and muscles came first and the bones later, but in the world to come the bones will come first and the new person will be re-created from the inside out. The school of Hillel said just the opposite, of course, saying that the process will be just the same in this world and the world to come. The skin and muscles will come first and the bones last in both. Does this remind you of any recent theological disputes? (*Genesis Rabbah* 14.5)

The young man driving the 1968 Chevrolet Impala was the namesake of one of the survivors of this "Trail of Tears," Ezekiel Dreadful Water, Zeke's great-great-grandfather. His forebear had been a Methodist lay preacher in the Indian Territories after the removal, and the old man's Bible had come to Zeke along with his name. Zeke's grandfather used to read to him from it just as his grandfather had done for him. The stories of the children of Israel were so intermingled with the memories of his own people that sometimes it was difficult for

Zeke to sort out which story appeared in the Bible and which did not. Not that it mattered much, since Zeke was not religious in any recognizable sense of the word. Neither did he go to church nor did he follow the old ways. Like every other Cherokee he knew, he saw the sacred nature of almost everything and everyone he encountered, but that was just ordinary life as he knew it, not something he could isolate and call his religion.

As he drove through the countryside of Middle Tennessee a memory kept surfacing that he could not quite put out of his mind. His grandfather had told him that his own grandfather had told of the many people who died along the trail of the removal. It always reminded the old preacher of the story in Ezekiel about the valley filled with dry bones. When he arrived in the Indian Territories he kept asking himself and God the question, "Can these bones live?"

"Did he ever answer the question?" Zeke would ask his grandfather. "You are the answer, my child," was his grandfather's reply, "and I am the answer. We live—the people live—as long as we remember."

Well, Zeke remembered alright, but he wasn't sure that what he pieced together of his family and tribal history was really an answer. The people didn't seem to be doing so well recently, if they ever had. After the War Between the States the Federal government would use the Native Americans' alliance with the Confederacy as justification for breaking treaties and taking what they wanted once again.

Each mile he drove became an endurance test, since he knew he was driving over the bones of his ancestors, the dry, dead bones of his past. Could these bones live? Not likely. He was not even sure what had drawn him to this grim pilgrimage; an old story told in an old book owned by an old man. Was that it? Was that the reason he found himself here rushing across sacred ground, throwing away the stealth of his hunter ancestors. As he accelerated, pushing his V8 past the legal speed limit, he could not escape the voices. His own voice blended with those of his ancestors and perhaps the Great Mystery, too. "Brother of earth, will these bones live?" *(Michael E. Williams)*

A Gourd and a Worm

Jonah preaches, Ninevah repents, and Jonah accuses God of compassion.

The Story

A second time the word of the LORD came to Jonah: 'Go to the great city of Nineveh; go and denounce it in the words I give you.' Jonah obeyed and went at once to Ninevah. It was a vast city, three days' journey across, and Jonah began by going a day's journey into it. Then he proclaimed: 'In forty days Ninevah will be overthrown!'

This greatly displeased Jonah. In anger he prayed to the LORD: 'It is just as I feared, LORD, when I was still in my own country, and it was to forestall this that I tried to escape to Tarshish. I knew that you are a gracious and compassionate God, long-suffering, ever constant, always ready to relent and not inflict punishment. Now take away my life, LORD: I should be better dead than alive.' 'Are you right to be angry?' said the LORD.

Jonah went out and sat down to the east of Ninevah, where he made himself a shelter and sat in its shade, waiting to see what would happen in the city. The LORD God ordained that a climbing gourd should grow up above Jonah's head to throw its shade over him and relieve his discomfort, and he was very glad of it. But at dawn the next day God ordained that a worm should attack the gourd, and it withered; and when the sun came up God ordained that a scorching wind should blow from the east. The sun beat down on Jonah's head till he grew faint, and he prayed for death; 'I should be better dead than alive,' he said. At this God asked, 'Are you right to be angry over the gourd?' 'Yes,' Jonah replied, 'mortally angry!' But the LORD said, 'You are sorry about the gourd, though you did not have the trouble of growing it, a plant which came up one night and died the next. And should not I be sorry about the great city of Nineveh, with its hundred and twenty thousand people who cannot tell their right hand from their left, as well as cattle without number?'

Comments on the Story

Two different lectionary readings are taken from these two chapters of Jonah. Jonah 3:1-5, 10 appears on the Third Sunday after Epiphany in year B. Jonah 3:10–4:11 is the reading on the Sunday of Ordinary Time Proper 20 [25] in year A, where it is read in conjunction with Matthew 20:1-16, the parable of the laborers in the vineyard.

It would be difficult to find in the Old Testament a book that should more delight a storyteller.

The genre of literature that Jonah represents is debated and probably will remain so. Everyone should be sure to enjoy the enormously humorous exaggerations in the telling of this story. The prophet is hardly your ideal prophet; the sailors are hardly stereotypical sailors; and the sinful inhabitants of Nineveh repent at the drop of a hat. Even God, who is supposed to be above the hustle of human behavior runs after the non-prophet Jonah, and later does an about-face on an important decree.

The third chapter puts the audience right in the middle of the story. Jonah has already unsuccessfully tried to escape the God who had given him a mission. Shipwreck, great-fish swallowing, and even being vomited out from the fish have already occurred, but they have not yet undone Jonah. It will be the unpredictable God and the curious Ninevites who will do that task in various roles and in surprising ways.

As a lectionary reading, 3:1-5 and 10 seem to want to point out Jonah's willingness (at last!) to do the bidding of God. Certainly the readiness of the Ninevites is something to be wondered at. The story has a connection with the books of Kings where there is a Jonah ben Amittai (2 Kings 14:25). Here, as well as there, the people's goodness is dependent on the goodness of their king. Lucky for them they have a good responsive king.

What is one to make of the king's decree that all people repent along with their animals? Animals as such play little role in the biblical texts with the exception of the book of Proverbs. The book of Proverbs occasionally holds up specific animals as examples to be emulated by human beings who want to make something out of their lives.

But here the animals participate fully in the fast from food and water that the humans do. One might understand the mention of the beasts in the call to repentance as a slip of the pen by the writer of the text. The excitement of the story might have carried away the writer to include the animals unthinkingly in the rite of penitence. (No one with any imagination can resist picturing a dog or a cow, robed in sackcloth, which now decides to "turn from its evil ways" and from "the violence in its hands.") But the reappearance of these animals in the last phrase of the book seems to endorse the possibility that the author had deliberately intended the animals in the city's relation to God. (The word that appears last in Hebrew is in English the word "many." One might say the author wanted the reader to be left with that very idea of many animals.)

After the prophet's initial positive response and the inhabitants' overwhelming positive response, Jonah behaves in a fashion that many find difficult to analyze. Is he angry, or disappointed? Does he feel cheated, disheartened, or revengeful? There seem to be many possibilities for what Jonah is thinking, in addition to what he says about wanting death and about the mercy and love of God.

Is he worrying about himself and his reputation as a prophet who foretold the city's downfall, but was thwarted by the inhabitant's repentance? Does this nonfulfillment of his prediction depress him? Is he worrying about a world where crime and sin go unpunished? Is he jealous of the easy life and reward the Ninevites received and the difficulty he has experienced? Is he angry over the loss of his one alleviation, the plant?

Perhaps the depiction of God is where the author invites us to focus. God certainly is depicted in the story as a God that does not have the limited view that might be charged to his depiction in many passages in the Old Testament. The God of the book of Jonah not only gets around, but moreover, has human beings and other elements within creation do his divine bidding. This God is concerned with other people more than the designated "chosen ones." Whether it is Mediterranean sailors or people with homes in Mesopotamia, this God takes an interest in, and receives a response from, any and all, even when one wouldn't expect it. Whatever things are meant by this book, this theme is clear, and ought never be overlooked.

Retelling the Story

> Are you right to be angry? said the LORD.
> (Jonah 4:4)

God spoke to Jonah, the son of Amittai, saying, "Go to Ninevah, that huge city and tell them that I am disgusted by their behavior." Now, this was a very odd command since the Ninevites were the enemy of the rest of the world including Israel. It would be like someone today traveling to the capital city of their worst enemy to tell them that God was displeased with them.

So Jonah did the only sensible thing. He headed in the opposite direction from Ninevah. He went down to the seacoast at Joppa, down to the shoreline, down into the dark hold of a ship, and finally down into the unconsciousness of sleep. This is clearly a downward slide for Jonah. He was headed for Tarshish, which was the other end of the earth in his day. But his plans were about to be changed.

God caused a storm to break loose on the Mediterranean and, in terror, the sailors began to do something very uncharacteristic for them: they started to pray to their various gods. Sailors are not noted for their piety. For example, you never hear anyone use the phrase, "To pray like a sailor." But I suppose there are no atheists in storms at sea just as there are none in foxholes. The captain finally came upon Jonah snoring through the storm and woke him, "Get up and pray to your God. Perhaps we can all be saved yet."

As in any crisis, someone had to be blamed. The sailors cast lots and the lot fell to Jonah. He confessed that he was trying to escape his God, the same one who had created heaven and earth, and the only remedy was to throw him overboard. The sailors rowed with all their might attempting to return the ship to shore, but to no avail. They finally threw Jonah overboard asking forgiveness for their action. As soon as he hit the water it became calm and the wind and the rain subsided. Seeing this dramatic turn of events, the ship's crew got religion and worshiped God. This is only the first of Jonah's great successes as a prophet and an evangelist.

When the storm arose and the ship on which Jonah had booked passage was about to be broken up, he confessed to the sailors that the storm was a result of his refusal to do what God had commanded him. The rabbis noted that the sailors attempted to return to shore before they decided to throw Jonah overboard. But the sages told that they went to even greater lengths to avoid tossing him into the water. First, they dipped him in up to his knees and the storm stopped. They breathed a sigh of relief and pulled him out again. The storm began again full force as soon as Jonah's feet cleared the water. The sailors kept dipping him; to his waist, his shoulders, his neck, and his nose. Each time the storm would stop as long as Jonah was in the water but began again as soon as he was taken out. Finally, there was nothing the sailors could do but throw him in. (Ginzberg IV, p. 248)

While the sailors were getting religion, Jonah was getting swallowed by a huge fish. Jonah spent three days in the fish's stomach, which was a dark, frightening, and smelly place. Jonah put together a prayer out of all the lines from prayers and psalms he could remember. Finally, God's water taxi had arrived at its destination and vomited Jonah upon the shore.

Once again, God told Jonah to go to Nineveh and what to tell the people there. This time Jonah headed straight for Nineveh. After walking one full day within the city, Jonah preached the shortest sermon on record. (Which may be the reason it was so effective!) He said, "In forty days Nineveh will be destroyed." Notice that he left the citizens no way out of their predicament.

Well, the most amazing thing happened. The entire city repented, from the king down to the poorest commoner. They all fasted and put on sackcloth and ashes to show how truly sorry they were for their behavior. Everyone living in the city repented in this fashion, *even the dogs, cats, and cattle.*

All this repenting really irked Jonah. Since he had gone to all the effort to proclaim destruction, he wanted to see the fireworks—an earthquake or raging fire that would consume his enemies as the fish had taken him in. "This is the very reason I tried to escape you in the first place," Jonah whined. Then the most successful prophet ever to utter a warning accused God, "I should have known you would pull something like this. After all, it's just like you—compassionate, slow to anger, merciful, always ready to forgive and reprieve people from the punishment they deserve. Just kill me right here on the spot. I'd be better off dead than alive anyway."

And God answered Jonah with this question, "What reason do you have to be so peeved?"

Jonah didn't answer, but went out to a place east of the city to sulk. Then God caused a castor-oil plant to spring up and shade the pouting prophet. (God's little joke, after all, Jonah was seriously retentive.) The next morning, however, God sent a worm to cut the plant down, and then sent the scorching sun and a hot wind from the east to heat up the situation. Once again Jonah proclaimed, "I would be better off dead than alive."

To which God replied with the same question that Jonah had refused to answer before, "What reason do you have to be so angry?"

"Every reason," Jonah snapped.

"You are more concerned about a plant than you are about all my people. But you had nothing to do with its springing up or its being cut down. It just grew one day and died the next. Shouldn't I have compassion on this great city with one hundred twenty thousand people who do not even know their right hand from their left as well as with the cattle which are too numerous to count?

Who does not know their right hand from their left? Small children and people of any age who have the minds of small children. Would God save an entire city for the sake of its children and animals? *(Michael E. Williams)*

> The repentance of the Ninevites was so profound that people who found that even one brick had been taken unjustly would tear down the entire structure to return that brick to its rightful owner. If someone found a treasure on a piece of property they had purchased from a neighbor they would attempt to return it to the person from whom they had bought the land. If neither of these could claim it, they both would seek among previous owners until the person to whom the treasure belonged, or his descendants, could be found. (Ginzberg IV, p. 251)

Into the Furnace

God will refine the people like fire refines gold.

The Story

I am about to send my messenger to clear a path before me. Suddenly the Lord whom you seek will come to his temple; the messenger of the covenant in whom you delight is here, here already, says the LORD of Hosts. Who can endure the day of his coming? Who can stand firm when he appears? He is like a refiner's fire, like a fuller's soap; he will take his seat, testing and purifying; he will purify the Levites and refine them like gold and silver, and so they will be fit to bring offerings to the LORD. Thus the offerings of Judah and Jerusalem will be pleasing to the LORD as they were in former days, in years long past.

Comments on the Story

This passage exhibits a new and distinctive way of conveying prophetic thought. The book of Malachi has six sections with this same new structure. A statement is made by the Lord, an objection is voiced by the people, and the prophet gives a divine assertion.

The book has the divine voice accusing the people of wearying the Lord. They have wearied the Lord by their claim that God sees evildoing as something that is good. And then they inconsistently claim that they sincerely ask about the existence and whereabouts of a just God.

Not truly clear is the intent of the statement in 2:17 that introduces our reading: "Every one who does evil is good in the sight of the Lord, and he delights in them." Also puzzling is the identity of the speaker who questions, "Where is the God of justice?"

The setting is a situation and a time in the postexilic period when the religious leaders, the priests, did not assume the full, traditional responsibility for the people. The bitter criticism, perhaps ironic only to a degree, cuts to the quick: you leaders have led the people astray. You have not lived up to the calling you received from God.

Then God responds, and this is where our reading begins. One would want the words reported as if from God to be clear and distinct. This reading begins with ambiguity. It continues with specifics and ends with clear hope based on a future purification.

The ambiguity begins already with the suffix on the Hebrew word for "messenger." The Hebrew has "my," while the earliest copies of the Greek translation have "his." So one can see ambiguity in the earliest textual traditions of this prophet.

One can point out that this Hebrew word, *mal'aki,* "my messenger," is identical to the name of the book of Malachi. Perhaps an editor thought that the prophet himself was the person that God was sending or had sent. The messenger might, however, be a different person, some human intermediary between God and the people. The divine angel or messenger could also be God, as it were, in disguise.

Added ambiguity is that the Hebrew of "the Lord" is neither of the usual two words that are mostly translated as "the Lord," namely, Yahweh or Adonai. Rather it is the simple word, *'adon,* which is often used when speaking of a human owner or powerful person. Perhaps this choice of word is a deliberate attempt to be sarcastic. This motivation would agree with the ironic sarcasm of the "whom you seek" and "in whom you delight." If these phrases refer to God, surely the people addressed do not truly seem to be sincere seekers.

As ambiguous, and perhaps more important, is the phrase, "the messenger of the covenant." There are at least three possibilities for the identity of the covenant. One possibility is the covenant of Sinai between Yahweh and Israel. Another covenant is that between God and David with his dynasty. Yet a third is the priestly covenant with the tribe of Levi and the Levitical priests.

The interest in priests in the book of Malachi is marked. Indeed, the focus on the temple as the destination for the coming of God does give weight to the priestly interpretation. There is a conceptual problem in the thought that God, who theoretically lives in the temple, will suddenly come to it. Perhaps that irony is overcome by the claim that Malachi, a critic of priests, might not have bought fully into the priestly idea of continuous divine presence in the temple.

Those readers familiar with Handel's *Messiah* might be troubled by the translation of the REB toward the end of 3:1. In Handel's music, the bass recitative sings "Behold, he shall come, saith the Lord of Hosts." (This occurrence of "the Lord" truly is the Hebrew "Yahweh.") The REB reads, "[He] is here, here already, says the Lord of Hosts." Hebrew tenses do not have the same unchanging meanings as English tenses. The REB differs from the KJV because it seems to interpret the messenger as the prophet.

The prophetic messenger is here to proclaim the day of God's coming. Malachi is the culmination of the prophetic tradition of "the day of the Lord." Different prophets gave a variety of emphases in their employment of the theme. Malachi returns to the original idea of salvation for God's people. But he sees that first a purification is needed.

God will come and sit down for the task of removing the impurities of the people whom the prophet compares to precious metals that need to be purified by fire. Curiously, the prophet also uses the comparison of wool that also needs preparation before it can be used as a garment. The prophet singles out the Levites as the particular group in need of this final attention.

Thus God is going to come and do the work of bringing to fulfillment the task begun long ago. God wants a faithful people, and God is willing to do the necessary work toward this fulfillment.

Retelling the Story

"[God's messenger] is like a refiner's fire, like a fuller's soap."
Malachi 3:2

Millie listened to the rhythm of her own footsteps as they tapped their way along Woodlawn Avenue. She was slower than last year, but there was still a liveliness in her step. The cold, still air in the dying sunlight of this December afternoon made everything sound more crisp than it would another day. As she approached the doors of the church, Millie hummed the chorus part to the piece she was going to rehearse; music she had known by heart for many years. She was glad to be going to rehearsal. In fact, she was glad to be going anywhere. Millie was just ecstatic about being alive.

She opened the heavy wooden doors by the large metal rings that served as door handles. The interior of the church was cool and dark, and a whisper of incense lingered throughout from the years of services that had been conducted there. The soloists were rehearsing as she entered, so Millie slipped into a pew and sat listening. She had always been in the chorus and had never even wanted to attempt to become a soloist. There was something very satisfying to her about blending into the crowd. She liked not standing out.

Danny Mandel, a middle-aged bass with a graying beard and a voice like thunder, was singing. She had worked with Danny before and loved hearing him sing. She did think he was too old to be called Danny. Daniel would have been more befitting someone with his obvious maturity and class. But then again she was just past seventy and was still called Millie, though she would never in a million years trade her childhood name for her given one, Mildred.

She had not yet regained her strength from her year-long ordeal. Those who had known her in previous productions mentioned to her that she had obviously lost weight. She did not go into the reasons, though they hardly left her consciousness for as much as a moment since her doctor's diagnosis had named her enemy. A mass they said and she almost laughed, for her first thought was of a worship service in this very sanctuary. From childhood she had grown up calling worship "the mass," though some modern Episcopalians used other terms these days.

But she did not laugh, because she knew what the young doctor meant, a mass in the right lung. No surgery. Perhaps chemotherapy or radiation. Add months, maybe years, to her life. Everything she remembered about that conversation after the word *mass* was a single word or phrase. There was not a single complete sentence among them. The chemotherapy had not caused her as much nausea as she had been led to believe. All her hair did fall out so that she took to wearing brightly colored turbans around the house and a rather nice wig when she went out. If she had realized how warm the wig was, she would have taken to wearing one in winter years ago.

The radiation had burned her esophagus so that for a time she could eat nothing solid and had to live on a liquid concoction that came in cans and was supposed to provide everything she needed. She knew, however, that no can of liquid nutrition or any doctor could provide everything she needed now. She simply took everything day by day and did anything she felt like doing.

Danny was coming to the part about God's messenger being like a refiner's fire. She liked this part, but this year it had another meaning for her. Had it been a refiner's fire that was shot at the tattooed cross on her breastbone? It had destroyed the mass the doctor had said, so it was certainly a destroyer's fire. Was it a refiner's fire as well? This past year had certainly refined Millie's senses. She didn't take anything for granted anymore. The simplest sight or sound could thrill her. To enjoy a real meal had become a luxury now that she could eat solid food again.

No creature can withstand the power of God's presence when the Creator of all the universe is pleased; then who could possibly survive God's displeasure? The awesomeness of the divine presence is overwhelming either way. But I, for one, would rather be overwhelmed by God's pleasure, if I had my choice. *(Exodus Rabbah 29.9)*

She remembered reading the passage from Malachi from which Handel had taken this portion of his masterpiece. Another line stuck in her memory, a question that had no answer, at least no answer she could form out of words. The messenger is like a refiner's fire, all right, but who could endure the day of his coming? Who could endure, she thought as Danny's voice pulsed through the floor, the pew, and her body. Who could endure? *(Michael E. Williams)*

182

A Joyful Return

God leads the people back into the joy of Jerusalem.

The Story

Jerusalem, strip off your garment of
    mourning and affliction,
and put on for ever the glorious
    majesty, the gift of God.
Wrap about you his robe of
    righteousness;
place on your head as a diadem the
    splendour of the Eternal.
God will show your radiance to every
    land under heaven;
from him you will receive for ever
    the name
Righteous Peace, the Splendour of
    Godliness.
Arise, Jerusalem, stand on the height;
look eastwards and see your children
    assembled
from west to east at the word of the
    Holy One,
rejoicing that God has remembered
    them.

They went away from you on foot,
led off by their enemies;
but God is bringing them home to you,
borne aloft in glory, as on a royal
    throne.
All the high mountains and
    everlasting hills
are to be made low as God
    commanded,
and every ravine is to be filled and
    levelled,
that Israel may walk securely in the
    glory of God;
and the woods and every fragrant tree
will give Israel shade at God's
    command.
He will lead Israel with joy
by the light of his glory,
in his mercy and his righteousness.

Comments on the Story

The book of Baruch does not appear to all scholars to be a unified composition. It could, rather, be a collection of somewhat disparate parts. This passage comes after a speech about wisdom which is in the form of an address to Israel.

This passage is grammatically addressed to Jerusalem. The difference is easy to see. Israel is the *people* of God, while Jerusalem or Zion is the *city* of God. All the prophets have used both ways of addressing the people in their oracles. And if one is reading a Hebrew text, those differences are always clear and even emphasized by the difference in grammatical gender. Grammatical gender is an aspect of language that Hebrew, by having verb forms that change according to gender, highlights more than English does. Israel is masculine and Zion/Jerusalem is feminine.

Many scholars judge that the original language of this part of Baruch was Hebrew or Aramaic. The earliest manuscripts we have of Baruch are in Greek. There is one fragment from chapter 6 among the Dead Sea Scrolls in Greek.

The storyteller uses the second half of the passage, the first half of which addresses Jerusalem as a mother whose children had been taken away and enslaved. She is told that joy is coming to her from the East, from God. Her sons and daughters will return to her and she shall rejoice.

The second half of the passage, our reading, continues that idea of rejoicing, and adds to it a kind of ceremony that Jerusalem performs by exchanging her old robe of mourning for the splendor of glory and the cloak of justice.

The writer of this piece is heavily influenced by the ideas and language of Second Isaiah. The exilic prophet wrote his comforting oracles in a time of difficulty during the Babylonian captivity. This writer has the task of writing in a different time, perhaps in a time of political freedom after the Maccabean revolt. But it could be that this part of the book was written when the Romans were just beginning to occupy the land of Israel (in the mid-first century B.C.E.), and there was little obvious hope of the Romans leaving.

Jerusalem is addressed and told to deck herself in finery to show the joy she experiences, just as she is told to do in Isaiah 52:1 and 61:10. One can almost see the now older woman who is widowed and is told that her children, whom she has not seen for many years, will now come back and see her. Her new attire will demonstrate the joy she feels.

Two terms by which the author refers to God in this section are remarkable, "the Eternal" (5:2) and "the Holy One" (5:5). These abstract terms are not found without some concrete reference in the Hebrew text of the Old Testament. Thus, rather than "the Holy One," the reader finds "the Holy One of Israel," a title that reminds the reader of the historical encounter between Israel and God over the course of its history. And the term translated "the Everlasting God" (Genesis 21:33) means more precisely the God whose limits one cannot know.

Striking too is the idea that Jerusalem's brilliance will be shown "to every land under heaven" (5:3). There is a beginning of universalism in the Hebrew Bible that is expressed usually in times of crisis and ambiguity. In the exile, Second Isaiah has God cry out, "I am the LORD, and there is none other; apart from me there is no god" (Isaiah 45:5).

Probably not surprising is the announcement of a change in Jerusalem's name. Many prophets declare that this city's name will be changed. Perhaps part of the reason for that is that all the prophets recognize that the ancient name "Jerusalem" bears a foreign god's name, for the name means "foundation of Shalem." The new names always eliminate that god. Baruch's new names both seem to have words that in Hebrew have been long connected with the ancient city traditions. "Righteous Peace" in Hebrew would be *Shalom Zedek,* and "Splendor of Godliness" could be *Kabod Hesed.* These four Hebrew words occur frequently in the Hebrew Bible in connection with Jerusalem.

There is one other writing that this passage is deeply indebted to, the Eleventh of the Psalms of Solomon, a work of the first century B.C.E. "Stand on the height," God "flattening the mountains," and the woods and trees shading Israel are expressions that are found within three lines of each other in the psalm. Baruch's writer knew the literature of his day and used it.

The passage, then, uses many ideas from previous and contemporary writings to give confidence and hope to a people who are conscious of their sinfulness and who need to be convinced of the graciousness of God and of the fulfillment that life with God will bring.

Retelling the Story

Jerusha had awaited this day for years, though she did not know it until a few months ago. Although she would turn eighty-six today, she was as excited as a little girl when visitors are coming. But these were not just visitors. These were her babies, whom she had not seen since they were children in 1943.

It seems odd to think of middle-aged men and women as babies, but that was the very word that came to her mind each time she thought of them. Would she even recognize them? She didn't know. But she would *know* them, Jerusha was sure of that. She hoped they would know her too.

For almost fifty years she had assumed they were dead, her David and Rachel, her Martin and Shira.

> The Baruch whose name is given to this book was assumed by many to have been the same Baruch who served as Jeremiah's secretary and disciple. While this is historically far-fetched, it made for some interesting stories about this character. For example, some sages believed that Baruch was one of only a few mortals to have visited paradise while still living. While he was grieving over the destruction of Jerusalem, a messenger of God took him on a tour of the judgment seat and the world to come. (Ginzberg IV, p. 323)

The last time she had seen them was when they had all been herded like so many cattle from the train at the so-called "labor camp." Then the Nazi guards had deprived her of everything dear to her: her parents, her husband, even her babies—or so she had believed until six months ago. Within hours, her tiny apartment in Jerusalem would be filled with voices and laughter, and most likely tears as well. But these would be tears of joy and remembrance.

Today her babies were coming home. She had bought a new dress for the occasion. She realized that this place had never been "home" to them. Their homes had been England, Argentina, and the United States, the countries in which the families who adopted them were living at the time. Slowly, over the years they had found each other, then decades later they had found her. One day a letter arrived, then the next day two more, and three days later a fourth. All her children had been alive all these years . . . alive, and she had not even known. They planned to arrive in Tel Aviv on the same day and appear at their mother's door together.

Israel had not been her home forever, either. After the war, she had drifted among so many other displaced persons, looking for any member of her family who might be alive. But she held out no hope. Finally, she was sponsored by several groups in Australia and moved there, married, but had no more children. After her Australian husband died, she had come to Jerusalem. Her grandfather had been a very pious man, a rabbi, whose fondest wish would have been to die in *Eretz Israel,* as he always called it. Had it been for him or for herself that she had moved? She could not say for sure. Now her apartment was as much home as any place in this world could be.

As she waited, fear mixed with the most intense expectation grasped her. Jerusha found herself doing the same task over and over again just to have something to do. She felt almost breathless with anticipation. She would know them and would love them, these babies whose lives had been ripped from her own. But could they love her? After all they had not seen her since they were just children. Would they blame her for not finding them, for not trying hard enough? She had tried, but during those dark days she could hardly bring herself to hope that they had survived; she knew of so many who had not. This was the best birthday gift ever for her. Whether it would be a gift for them she could not know.

It was said that Baruch was still alive when the exiles were allowed to return home. But his faithful disciple Ezra remained with him until his death. That was because Ezra believed that it was more important to study Torah than to rebuild the temple. So, say certain sages, it was only after Baruch died that the exiles returned. (Ginzberg IV, p. 323)

She heard footsteps in the hall, then a knock. She paused, then threw open the door. Outside were her grown-up babies, the best present ever, too good to hope for. They each said "Mama!" That word brought tears for Jerusha, tears for all the lost ones, and for these who had been found. She could hardly find her voice to say the words she had practiced so many times, "Welcome home." *(Michael E. Williams)*

Index of Readings
from the *Revised Common Lectionary*

188

Index
of Midrashim

Genesis Rabbah

Exodus Rabbah

Leviticus Rabbah

Numbers Rabbah

Ecclesiastes Rabbah

1.4 [4]	135	7.27 [1]	75

Song of Songs Rabbah

1.2 [3]	86	3.11 [2]	72
2.2 [6]	112	6.11 [1]	112
3.4 [2]	56		

Sefer Ha-Aggadah

6.5	52	463.567	93
150.20	27	476.73	143
198.21	139	497.98	167
245.194	154	506.225	128
292.491	63	510.52	40
306.13	39	554.172	35
393.40	99	556.195	155
393.41	104	557.207	160
394.47	47	666.262	98
396.56	103	708.211	110
399.1	127	717.310	81
404.22	86	770.110	47
434.306	63	792.27	140
456.509	171